"Echo Huang is a consummate professional and world-class investment advisor. This comprehensive financial guidebook is the result of years and years of hands-on experience, observation, and learning. Her broad and deep knowledge of the complex intricacies of financial planning shines through, and it is abundantly evident that Echo is not only a CERTIFIED FINANCIAL PLANNER™ (CFP) Professional, but also a CPA and Chartered Financial Analyst (CFA) charterholder. Though her book demonstrates mastery of technical detail and financial savvy, what is perhaps most impressive is her passion and caring for guiding individuals through the complex maze that is financial planning. Furthermore, Echo walks the talk, as she is the living embodiment of the 'American dream'—in her financial advisory practice and in her personal life."

Clayton W. Chan, Esq.
Chan, PLLC, Law Offices, Estate Planning

"Growing up in a small village in China, Echo Huang had dreams of traveling the world. Through her formal education and corporate experience, but more so through her drive and tenacity, Echo gained in-depth knowledge of wealth and tax planning techniques while also developing the principles that guide her decisions. Echo's book, Own Your Future: One Woman's Story of Immigration and Financial Freedom, *is the perfect mix of storytelling, inspiration, practical advice, and can-do attitude that will propel its readers to write their own stories of financial strength."*

Cory Kiner
CPA, E.T. Kelly & Associates, LLC

"The courageous journey of a woman who 'dared to dream' and from humble beginnings has become a top-rated wealth management leader. Seizing every opportunity for development and finding her sweet spot led to her own financial independence. Own Your Future *helps demystify the sometimes scary investment world with helpful guidance, easy to follow steps, and wise all-around financial counsel. A must-read if you want financial peace of mind and a 'return on life.'"*

Tito Wouda
VP of finance, General Mills, Inc.

"After reading this book, I immediately gave it to my twenty-one-year-old daughter, who will be graduating from college this coming spring. Not only does this work provide an outstanding introduction to the strategies and tactics of personal finance, but it is also full of fascinating and personal stories of how a young woman realized her dreams by developing a series of personal principles. This is a book for anyone who can use both deep insight and many practical tools to develop a self-directed and independent future."

Barrie Froseth, PhD
Retired, General Mills, Inc.

"Echo has a rare combination of technical expertise and empathy. This enables her to provide a unique perspective on wealth management that is both informative and motivating!"

Jerry Young, *Retired controller, General Mills, Inc.*
Julia Young, *Former finance manager, General Mills, Inc.*

OWN

YOUR

future

ONE WOMAN'S STORY
of IMMIGRATION *and*
FINANCIAL FREEDOM

OWN
YOUR
future

ECHO HUANG
CFA, CFP®, CPA

Advantage

Published by Advantage, Charleston, South Carolina.
Member of Advantage Media Group.

ADVANTAGE is a registered trademark, and the Advantage colophon is a trademark of Advantage Media Group, Inc.

Printed in the United States of America.

10 9 8 7 6 5 4 3 2 1

ISBN: 978-1-64225-088-6
LCCN: 2020901790

Cover design by Megan Elger.
Layout design by Jennifer L. Witzke.

This publication is designed to provide accurate and authoritative information in regard to the subject matter covered. It is sold with the understanding that the publisher is not engaged in rendering legal, accounting, or other professional services. If legal advice or other expert assistance is required, the services of a competent professional person should be sought.

Advantage Media Group is proud to be a part of the Tree Neutral® program. Tree Neutral offsets the number of trees consumed in the production and printing of this book by taking proactive steps such as planting trees in direct proportion to the number of trees used to print books. To learn more about Tree Neutral, please visit **www.treeneutral.com**.

Advantage Media Group is a publisher of business, self-improvement, and professional development books and online learning. We help entrepreneurs, business leaders, and professionals share their Stories, Passion, and Knowledge to help others Learn & Grow. Do you have a manuscript or book idea that you would like us to consider for publishing? Please visit **advantagefamily.com** or call **1.866.775.1696**.

***To my mom, Huiying**, who has given me intelligence and the courage to try new things: There's no way I can pay you back, and I cherish the time we spend together.*

***To my only child, Nina**, who is talented and imaginative: I want you to know where you came from, and you have all the power you need to accomplish whatever you dream. I love you always.*

CONTENTS

FOREWORD

Echo is an amazing role model for all of us. She is my favorite example of someone who has vision to see the future, owns her personal choices, and makes things happen.

She starts with her personal history, where she traces a path from China to the United States. We learn what turned her into a woman of action instead of one who just lets things happen to her. Strong forces of economic reform swirled around her family in the 1980s. Her mother's Russian language skills pulled them out of the agrarian countryside into the newly created Special Economic Zone in Shenzhen. Echo also discovered the travel writings of Sanmao or Echo Chan, a female Taiwanese author, who inspired her to dream of the greater world. All of this opened opportunities to a young woman with "intelligence and the courage to try new things."

She learned how to dare to dream, respect education, set goals, and make plans while remaining adaptable. She always works to improve her position and learn lessons along the way in order to be ready to seize the next opportunity. She also values the wisdom of others. We can all learn from these guiding principles.

I love the clear and transparent approach that she provides to wealth management in this book. She starts with the honest understanding that the industry can make things more complex than they need to be—which can be especially off-putting for women, especially those that did not have the loving inspiration of Echo's mother and the writings of Echo Chan to shape their self-confidence.

Echo unveils the industry's secrets one by one in a simple fashion. She shares why it is important to understand your current starting point, to review current spending patterns, and to identify goals before making a recommendation. She shows how tools like the Echo Dashboard can make your financial outlook transparent, for today's details and for your long-term trajectory. She teaches us about the common behavioral biases that can get in the way of our goals and how important it is to ensure that short-term beliefs, emotions, and impulses don't impact long-term investments with the help of the steady hand of a trusted advisor.

One of her goals is to educate and inspire more people to start planning now to own their future, as well as to inspire other women to join the profession. Echo breaks it apart into the basics and provides true insight into what will make a difference. Not for just anyone. For you. Your dreams. Your situation. I am positive that it will give you the confidence to follow your dreams!

As someone in a common circle of trust, I benefit from her candid questions. "Natalie, what do you want out of your life? Are you optimizing your choices? How are you following up on this dream?" She regularly reminds me to be intentional in the choices that I make. It is such a gift to have this in my life—a wonderful gift that she shares with you in *Own Your Future*.

—Natalie Doyle, *senior vice president, Aristocrat*

INTRODUCTION

The term "wealth management" doesn't only apply to wealthy people. You don't have to be wealthy to start managing wealth; you can start growing it now from right where you stand. Too many people don't understand the roles and responsibilities of financial advisors or financial planners and therefore fail to take advantage of opportunities to grow their wealth. Some financial advice books are too complicated, and others are a little too basic, but this book aims to give you the tools and education to think properly about your money, to identify who should be on your financial team, and to offer insights into what each of them should deliver. As you'll see in chapter 3, wealth management can be complicated, but it doesn't have to be.

This book is a natural extension of the blog I began three years ago to educate people about wealth management and offer useful tools that can be used to make financial life more organized. Over time, it became apparent that there was a need to compile this information into one book that presented each step of the process. In the following pages, I will be pulling back the curtain on the profession as a whole and showing you how to make it work for you as well as whom and what to trust. We have all heard about investment managers who have done wrong by their clients. While these

1

scoundrels make the news, they are thankfully few and far between. Today, the CERTIFIED FINANCIAL PLANNER (CFP®) designation requires holders to have undergone about two to three years of study and three years of working experience in financial planning.[1]

This book will show you who should be on your team, what the responsibilities of each are, and how they should be working together in a holistic way to help you reach your financial independence day. Additionally, for those interested in a career in finance, I will show that it is possible to have a successful career doing what you love and still be kind and ethical.

In the following chapters, I will be sharing my story and my background—how I was born in a poor village in China with no running water, how I had dreams that nobody else could understand, and how I learned that anything is possible if you set your mind to it. The first chapter describes the formative lessons I learned in life and shares that knowledge with you. Chapter 2 recounts my early experiences in the United States, my new learning opportunities, and the processes of solidifying of my values of meticulous planning, daring to dream, seizing opportunities as they arose, and creating opportunities to network. I'll look at different steps that can be taken to help you find solutions to any problems you face.

Chapter 3 begins our look at financial planning and shows that wealth management can be complicated but doesn't have to be. Chapter 4 explores behavioral biases and how to recognize them and make behavioral and attitudinal adjustments to create a better future. Chapter 5 then explains how you can achieve your financial independence day by setting goals that will help you prepare for retirement, what questions to ask yourself, and what plans to make in order to

---

1 The Financial Planning Association has a directory of qualified professionals and holds each to a recognized standard of excellence for competent and ethical personal financial planning. See http://www.plannersearch.org for more information.

put a date on the calendar to declare: "This is my financial independence day." In chapter 6, we look at investment planning, including risk tolerance and how to think about investing from a global perspective. Chapter 7 takes a look at your dream team, who should be on that team, and how they should be working together.

The next chapters look at your current financial situation. Chapter 8 looks at tax strategies and offers tips on what you should consider in your tax plan. Chapter 9 looks at what estate planning is and why it's an important part of your overall financial plan. It will ask some questions that you need to think about, such as what should be included in your estate plan and when you should seek professional help. Chapter 10 examines long-term care, what it is, and why it should be part of your overall plan. It also suggests questions to consider when devising this plan and what type of advisor you should turn to for help when needed.

Finally, chapter 11 looks at charitable giving, not only why it can work for you in terms of efficient tax strategies, but also in terms of giving back to people in need and using this as a way to enhance quality of life for yourself and also for the beneficiaries. Chapter 12 summarizes and concludes the book.

The following pages will show that just because you may be in a difficult situation one day, this doesn't mean you will be there forever. This was important for me to recognize as I was growing up with the restrictions of mainland China. The key was finding role models and reading many books to learn ways to move forward. I have benefited from some great inspirers and influencers on my journey.

I have three purposes in writing this book. The first is to educate and inspire more people to start planning now to own their futures. The second is to reveal how wealth management is done by a fiduciary financial planner so that readers can decide how to choose the right financial planner to partner with. The third is to encourage more women to choose this profession to address women's unique challenges. On my path, two women in particular have had a great influence on me. They have in turn inspired me to influence other women in a positive way, especially those who are thinking about a career in wealth management or those who are struggling to manage their finances. Traditionally, financial services has been a male-dominated industry; even making financial decisions in the home has traditionally fallen onto men. In the following pages, I hope to show women that they can not only step out and become financial planners, but they also can actually take a very proactive role in managing their own finances to achieve their dreams and create the kind of quality of life that they want.

Own Your Future: One Woman's Story of Immigration and Financial Freedom is the story of how a poor immigrant came to live the American dream and how you can too. It tells my story of how success came as a result of resilience, vision, and gaining wisdom by surrounding myself with inspiring individuals. It's a story of dreams manifested as a result of the guidance offered by my seven core principles: daring to dream, being adaptable, respecting education, setting goals, utilizing smart and deliberate planning to achieve success, seizing opportunities when they arise, and benefiting from the wisdom of others.

After accumulating over twenty years' experience in the trenches, not just in investment management but also in private and public accounting, I am confident the following pages will be educational and useful for your financial planning goals and hope that many of the principles and stories I share will give you new ideas or at least encourage you to try something new that has the potential to improve not only your portfolio, but also your life.

CHAPTER 1

Echoes of China

Growing up in a poor village in the People's Republic of China was a world away from my life today in the United States. Back then, my dream to travel the world was a source of amusement for the rest of the village, where few people made it as far as high school and even fewer moved away from the place they were born. No one from my village would believe the story of my life: how I moved with my family at twelve years old to Shenzhen, where I finished school and got a great job in a bank, which was the envy of my childhood friends, or how I later managed to find a way out of China to arrive in the United States with only $800 in my pocket and a place in an undergrad finance program at an American university. No one could have dreamed that it was possible to go from running to school through snake- and leech-infested rice paddy fields in rural China to being a five-star wealth manager with over $100 million assets under management in a major US city within twenty-seven years. No one, that is, except me.

Early Life and First Guiding Principles

From my earliest days, I yearned to see the sky from different places all over the globe. This is why Xintian, which is Chinese for New Skies, was an appropriate name for the village in which I was born in 1971. Traveling the world was a pie-in-the-sky dream for a young girl in a poor village in the southern part of the People's Republic of China, where we had neither the money to take a vacation to the next town nor the political freedom to leave the country, but I still looked at a map and said, "Someday I will travel around the world." The other villagers laughed at me, but I was determined somehow, someday, to fulfill my dream. My first guiding principle, therefore, was formed at an early age: dare to dream.

GUIDING PRINCIPLE 1

Dare to dream. Sometimes we have to be daring to dream. A crazy goal will help you extend your reach. During my teenage years, the globe-trotting female Taiwanese writer Sanmao opened my eyes even more to this idea. She was proof of the importance of finding your inspiration, daring to follow your dreams, and refusing to allow others to dampen them.

The village where I lived in my early years (Jiantou) was small by Chinese standards. There was no reliable electricity, and we had to get water from wells. People built small one-story houses out of mud bricks that farmers made from the soil in their fields by using sticky mud, stacked and dried to make very large blocks.

I was fortunate to have a little more than most other kids in that rural village; this was because my parents had college degrees, and their housing was provided by the school. They each had a steady salary, and we had enough to eat and nice clothes, including skirts that my father and mother made together.

The other villagers were farmers or laborers of some kind, which meant that most of the time, they were growing vegetables and rice. We were surrounded by rice paddy fields. Every day, the village farmers waded through these fields, up to their knees in mud. They harnessed water buffalo to plough the marshy fields. None of these farmers could afford modern equipment. Water buffaloes were their tools, not tractors. Once finished with plowing, these farmers had to transplant the rice seedlings to the rice paddy fields once they showed three to four leaves, which was made all the more arduous because of the leeches that infested the waters into which they waded up to their knees. I was more afraid of snakes than leeches. The subtropical climate was heaven for snakes. They would just appear on the path, slithering along in front of me. Every morning, I ran to school as fast as I could through those paddy fields.

There were no televisions in our village, but some people had battery-powered radios. These were our only connections to the outside world and world affairs. Bigger villages had outdoor movie theaters, where people could watch black-and-white movies, which were usually government propaganda films. Other than that, we were very isolated.

For a child, however, it was a happy life. We didn't have much to worry about. We had very few toys, but we had plenty of trees to climb. We made candles using bamboo by putting a string into its hollow center and pouring wax around it. We made kites using old newspapers. We didn't have glue, so we used sticky rice as glue and then tied the kites with thin strips of bamboo. Necessity, they say, is the mother of invention, which was why, from a very young age, I learned to respond to circumstances by being inventive and adaptable. Therefore, early in life, adaptability became the second of my guiding principles.

GUIDING PRINCIPLE 2

Be adaptable. Even the most deliberate and best-laid plans need some flexibility. Always be adaptable.

Sociopolitical Climate and New Guiding Principles

When I was a child, the state supplied schooling up to middle school. Most Chinese children could go to these state-run schools if their parents wanted them to have some education. It wasn't mandatory that they attend, and many didn't because their families needed them to work on the farm. This meant anyone who finished middle school was doing well, but education largely stopped there. Few families could sacrifice farm work to education. Fortunately, our family was different.

My maternal grandmother, Jingtai, grew vegetables and rice to support the family—this was something everyone had to do in those days to support themselves—but her main source of income was from midwifery, which she learned from her mother. She was born in 1909 when no women in poor villages could go to school. She was illiterate until my mother taught her how to read and write much later in life. Her midwifery skills were greatly valued by others, as was she for being brave and diligent, especially for trying new ways to revive sick babies. Her courage was instilled in my mother and me in turn.

My maternal grandfather, who had a school maintenance job, passed away when my mother was in high school. My mother was top of her class and had ambitions to go to college, even though sending a girl to college was very unusual in those days when society favored boys over girls. However, in a family imbued with a willingness to make any sacrifice for education, my two elder uncles rallied to support my mother in finishing her education. Her determination to get an education paved the way for me to later realize my dreams. The success she achieved as a result of deciding to focus on her education forged another of my guiding principles: respect for education. Her pivotal decision to forge ahead with her schooling would eventually get our family out of the paddy fields and ultimately allow me to become the successful financial services business owner I am today.

GUIDING PRINCIPLE 3

Respect education. Education means continuous learning. It doesn't stop when you graduate. It's important to constantly study to learn new skills and acquire more knowledge.

My parents met in 1969 while attending Huanan Teachers' College in Guangzhou, capital city of Guangdong Province. They married in 1970. I was born in 1971, and two sisters followed me in the next three years. This was before the one-child rule was implemented in China. In those days, the government decided where skills and diplomas were most needed and assigned people to those locations. As a result, my parents were assigned to teach in separate villages, and I lived with my mother and maternal grandmother in Jiantou, two hours away from my father, until I was eight years old.

Because my father had to remain two hours away to teach in his village, my grandmother lived with us to help my mother, who had a full-time job as an English teacher, raise her children. As a result, my grandmother greatly influenced me.

My mother's pivotal decision to forge ahead with her schooling would eventually get our family out of the paddy fields and ultimately allow me to become the successful financial services business owner I am today.

She told me stories about the village in her dialect, Hakka, which was the only language I spoke until I learned Mandarin when I started school at six years old. I helped her grow vegetables and raise chickens for eggs. Eggs were a precious food, so much so that when I received a perfect score in an exam, my grandmother rewarded me with two eggs! Today, in Minnesota, my daughter Nina, who doesn't like eggs at all, thinks this is very funny.

Winning those eggs taught me a valuable lesson at a young age: it's important to set goals. On August 31, the night before a new school year, I would lie awake at night setting goals. Some goals were just to meet new kids. Later, these were to become the top student, who won two eggs. Setting goals was instilled in me from a young age and has steadied me through life ever since.

GUIDING PRINCIPLE 4

Set goals. The desire to set and achieve goals is key to knowing how to prepare and when to grasp opportunities as they arise.

Teenage Years and Final Guiding Principles

When I was eight years old, my parents moved to a bigger village called Lankou. They were finally able to work in the same school, and I was finally able to see my father every day. Lankou was a land of luxury compared to Jiantou. We had running water and electricity. For the first time, I saw a glimpse of modernity, and I wanted more. Four years later, at twelve years old, I got my wish when we made an even more transformative move to the city of Shenzhen.

My parents spent two years applying for jobs in Shenzhen. Opportunities were few in China and not to be squandered. It was hard to know what opportunities might arise because they were hard to come by within the restricted framework of life in China in those days; nevertheless, my parents persisted in preparing the groundwork to advance once a situation to do so arose. From this experience, I learned the importance of meticulous and deliberate preparation in order to be in a position to grasp an opportunity when it arose. This is how I later managed to graduate from college within three and a half years with a high GPA.

GUIDING PRINCIPLE 5

Meticulously prepare for every single thing. Set a goal and lay out a plan with different time frames and deadlines. As your plan advances, assess whether anything more can be done or any lessons can be applied.

In the early 1980s, people called Chinese politician Deng Xiaoping "the architect" of a new brand of thinking that combined socialist ideology with pragmatic market economy. He made Shenzhen the first Special Economic Zone (SEZ) in China. This was a form of capitalism within the socialist society. He offered different tax incentives within this zone to attract foreign investment. His policy of "reform and opening up" transformed what had been a small fishing village on the border of Hong Kong with a population of less than fifty thousand people, to a major city in Guangdong Province of twenty million, and from small one-story houses to sky-scrapers similar to those of Hong Kong. Deng had a huge effect on Chinese people in terms of lifting them out of poverty. It was one of the fastest-growing cities in the world in the 1990s and 2000s.[2] It hosts the Shenzhen Stock Exchange as well as the headquarters of

2 "Shenzhen," US Commercial Service (2007). Available at http://webarchive.loc.gov/all/20150412050558/http%3A/export.gov/china/doingbizinchina/regionalinfo/second-tiercities/eg_cn_025695.asp.

numerous multinational companies. It's also a leading global technology hub, often called the next Silicon Valley.[3]

My parents could see that Shenzhen was the place to be, but regulations within the education system as well as government control made it very difficult to move. It took a lot of effort to go through the levels of authority to get the ear of someone who could made decisions. It wasn't enough to plead that the move would be good for you; you had to convince those in authority that the move would be good for others too. This meant they needed to demonstrate some kind of uniqueness or special talent.

For my mother, this turned out to be the Russian language. In 1983, the burgeoning city needed teachers to help it modernize. My mother had been teaching Chinese, math, singing, and English in a small village, and my father had taught physics before being promoted to principal. My mother had majored in Russian in college but never had a single Russian student. Living in a small village a thousand miles from Russia, she had never even met a Russian. However, having this language expertise made her application stand out, so she persisted until she convinced someone that she had a unique skill set that justified her move to the city. My father was also given a job in the same school, Futian Middle School.

I give my parents a lot of credit for driving so hard to get those jobs in such restrictive circumstances. Their story evinces what I tell people I meet in major US cities today—that one of the keys to success is seizing opportunities as they arise.

---

3 Tobias Kremkau, "The next Silicon Valley? It could be here," *Das Netz Online* (July 11, 2017). Available at http://dasnetz.online/en/the-next-silicon-valley-it-could-be-here/.

GUIDING PRINCIPLE 6

Seize opportunities. Almost all opportunities come with some risk, but risk can be mitigated by planning and calculation. Once you are prepared, it's important to seize every opportunity that arises.

My childhood friends were limited in terms of opportunities, but my parents' and grandparents' drive made sure that we got out of the village and into a global city where education and cultural exposure was possible. Their decisions benefited me greatly. They offered me a place from which I could jump off.

My mother taught me the importance of independence and preparation, even when we don't know what opportunities may appear. She taught me not to let an opportunity pass me by. All opportunities involve risk, but this can be a calculated risk. Often, you just need to be decisive and assess the risk as you go. My mother was also a great example of adaptability in the way she worked and planned her way out of rural life by positioning herself to move to Shenzhen. She is an independent woman who achieved success by being adaptable and learning new skills. My mother has always been a strong female role model. Without her actions and inspiration, I wouldn't have made it to college to study business or into the Bank of China later.

Principles in Practice

Moving to Shenzhen was exciting for a teenager who had come from a small village to a city of seventy thousand people. Enormous buildings were being constructed around the clock. Over the next twenty years, the city ballooned to fifteen million people, making it a metropolitan melting pot. From the antenna on our balcony, we got Hong Kong TV, which gave me some exposure to Western culture for the first time. Until then, I had only heard government propaganda on the radio in our village. Now, even though I couldn't cross the border to Hong Kong because at that time it was a British colony, I could climb to the top of my parents' apartment building and see a city that offered me a glimpse of the global stage.

Shenzhen renewed my commitment to my first principle by reviving my childhood dream to travel to far-flung regions of the world. It shook me out of the rural mind-set of the South China Communist state and made me savvy to the workings of capitalism and the Western world.

The move to Shenzhen, however, wasn't without challenges. My parents had three daughters born within four years, and while college tuition wasn't exorbitant, certainly not compared to the fees of an American university, the sundry items, such as books, travel, dormitories, and food, added up. In the village, my parents were comparably well off, but in Shenzhen, they were not. In this burgeoning commercial city, teachers didn't earn a lot of money, which meant having all three daughters in college in four-year degree programs would be a huge burden. I needed to find a solution to manifest my third principle of respecting education in order to succeed.

By the age of fourteen, I knew I wanted to go into business, mainly because I wanted to be independent and, as the firstborn child, I wanted to share the financial burden facing the family of raising two younger siblings. I decided to go to the Shenzhen School of Business and Economics, which offered a three-year diploma in accounting. This was financially manageable compared to the far more expensive path of going to senior high school, taking national exams, and going to university.

Thus, by being adaptable, I became a seventeen-year-old with a diploma in accounting in a city that desperately needed accountants. As a result, I landed a great job with the Bank of China in Shekou, a seaside town about thirty minutes away, earning more money than

I knew this was not where I belonged forever. I knew I could do better. It was just a matter of waiting for the right opportunity to arise.

my parents, who had college degrees. The Bank of China was the only bank in those days that handled foreign currency exchange, and working with foreign currency was quite an accomplishment for a seventeen-year-old. I put my English to use when helping foreign customers exchange currencies. In addition, the bank provided housing for employees, which gave me a great amount of independence at a young age.

When I was about nineteen, my mother and I went to visit a Western-style grocery store for the first time. They had nicely displayed Washington apples and grapes along with cheeses we'd never seen before. We didn't buy anything because it was so much more expensive than the food in Chinese markets. As we left the store, I said to my mother, "Someday I will bring you to this kind of grocery store, and you won't have to look at the prices at all. You'll be able to choose any food you want."

I made this promise because I was determined to be financially independent and help my family. This promise also motivated me to look for more opportunities. I knew the bank job wasn't the last step for me, far from it, but the next step had not been revealed. I knew this was not where I belonged forever. I knew I could do better. It was just a matter of waiting for the right opportunity to arise.

Owning the Future

In the early '90s in Shenzhen, I was growing unhappy with having only my diploma in accounting. I have never been one to settle, so as successful as I was at seventeen, I wanted more.

As a teenager, I began reading everything I could by Sanmao, a Taiwanese writer also known as Echo Chan, who wrote books about her travel experiences in over fifty countries. As a citizen of Taiwan, she was free to travel, unlike a Chinese citizen from mainland China. She blazed a trail that inspired me to keep moving. She showed me that I was able to do much more. I was so inspired by her life that not only was my childhood desire to travel the world fueled by her adventures, but I also took her name as my middle name when I came to the United States. Along with my grandmother and parents, I learned from reading Sanmao's work how much guidance was attainable by being willing to listen and absorb the wisdom of others.

GUIDING PRINCIPLE 7

Value the wisdom of others. An extraordinary amount of success can be achieved from the simple act of seeking out and being willing to listen to the guidance of others.

Sanmao inspired me to look for new opportunities, although few existed at that time in China. I knew I would have to look elsewhere. I wanted to study abroad, just like Sanmao, but since the mainland Chinese people couldn't leave the People's Republic of China, I had no idea how to make that happen. This was a time when my guiding principles became very important; not knowing how or when an opportunity would present itself didn't stop me from getting prepared for the day that it would. I knew on that day I would need to speak English, so I spent three years taking English classes after work.

My motivation to leave China was additionally fueled by a significant but negative incident in my life, which didn't take the form of an opportunity but was formative nevertheless.

The bank had given me an apartment on the second floor of a building. It had a door to a large outside balcony. I went to bed one very cold winter night, a few days before the Chinese New Year. I woke up suddenly under a weight on top of me. Within seconds, duct tape covered my mouth. With no moon that night, it was pitch black, and I couldn't see my attacker even though he was right on top of me, pressing his hand hard over my mouth. I struggled, and he fell to the floor. I leapt up, tore off the duct tape, and ran screaming to the door for help. He fled onto the balcony and disappeared. I heard a motorbike screeching away. I locked all the doors, and went back to my room to calm down. My lips were cut from the metal braces I wore at the time. My hand was cut in the struggle. It was then I saw a rope with a knot lying on the floor next to my bed. That situation could have been much worse. I could have been murdered.

I filed a police report but had very little to offer for evidence. For weeks, I lived in fear, suspecting all sorts of people I saw in passing. The perpetrator was never caught. I didn't tell my parents for fear they'd insist I move home. I didn't want to give the incident the power to move me backward. I loved my independence. I refused to be a victim to this assault. I wanted security, not just financial security but also physical security. Shenzhen, however, was changing for both good and bad, and I no longer felt safe there. I reexamined my goals and redoubled my efforts to find a way out.

Soon afterward, my uncle Yuanfa, who had supported my mother throughout her college years, became a visiting chemistry scholar on a two-year contract at the University of Idaho. He asked if I wanted to study finance in the United States while he was there. I was twenty years old and in a great job that most people would love to have. I was financially independent and living a great life, but I knew that if I didn't grab this opportunity to study in the United States, it would probably never come around again. This was my chance to get away, so I made a scary but pivotal decision to find a way to go overseas.

There were many obstacles to overcome to realize this goal. I didn't have a bachelor's degree, which meant I needed to apply for undergraduate study programs. Visas were generally issued for postgrad study. To stack the deck even more strongly against myself, I wanted to study finance in a country that was awash in finance degrees. I had little to offer by way of uniqueness to justify my place, but I wasn't prepared to give up. I needed to pass the Test of English as a Foreign Language (TOEFL), find a sponsor who lived outside of China, and be accepted by at least one university in the United States in order to apply for a passport and get an F1 full-time student visa. I also had to quit my good job, which was risky, but I had to apply own principles: plan and seize opportunities to push forward toward my goals. Many people who applied for the F1 visa at the US embassy in Guangzhou didn't get one, but my passion to learn new skills and my curiosity about the financial world convinced the female immigration officer that I wouldn't be a burden to the United States. When she said, "Welcome to America," I knew this day was one of the best days of my life.

On January 11, 1992, I flew from Hong Kong to Seattle and then took a Greyhound bus for eight hours to Moscow, Idaho. The trip was nerve-racking but exhilarating. I remembered how the villagers had once laughed at my dream to travel, and now here I was finally traveling halfway around the world. All I had was $800 in my pocket—not much in dollars, but it was a small fortune in

Chinese yuan—and high hopes for the future. I had been earning about eight hundred yuan per month at the Bank of China (about $100) in 1991 and saved for three years to pay for the airfare. Almost all of my parents' savings were in that $800, but mother was in tears at the Shenzhen train station, saying goodbye and wishing she could help me more. I comforted her by saying, "Mom, don't worry. You've given me the best gifts: a smart brain and the courage to try new things."

My first year in the United States wasn't easy for me. Despite all my preparation and planning, nothing in mainland China could have prepared me for life in the United States. Even though I had passed the TOEFL exam, I couldn't understand the economics professor and take good notes while attending my first class, macroeconomics. I had to read the entire chapter using an English-Chinese dictionary the night before the class in order to understand the lecture. I had to drop the English literature class after a week to change to geography because I simply couldn't read fast enough, especially old English. My $800 didn't last long. I stayed with my uncle and his family for my freshman year to save money. I worked in the dish room of the cafeteria on campus up to twenty hours per week for $4.25 per hour. I borrowed money from my uncle to cover fees and expenses, but it was soon obvious that no amount of loans or work would support me through the four-year degree program at the University of Idaho. As a foreign student, I couldn't apply for any student loans. My mother found two sponsors who lived outside of China in order for me to apply to other colleges and obtain a student visa. I didn't plan on asking the sponsors for money if I could work and obtain scholarships in the United States. I was $3,000 in debt at the end of the first year even though I didn't live in the dorm, worked twenty hours per week during the school year, and worked full time in the summer.

Total costs for a nonresident student were close to $10,000 per year. This was a huge amount of yuan, far too expensive for my family. It was time to incorporate another guiding principle: be adaptable. It was time to devise a new plan.

I heard that Winona State University in Minnesota was offering foreign students resident tuition if they had a 3.0 GPA and if they agreed to introduce their culture to its community. I had a 4.0 GPA. I applied and was accepted. I packed my bags and moved to Minnesota alone, without knowing anyone, in March 1993, ready to grasp this new opportunity.

At Winona State, I had to make further adjustments to my plan, but a new challenge presented itself. My visa only allowed me to work for one year after graduation to gain practical training, so making the most of employment opportunities was paramount. If I failed to find a job, I would have to return to China with no work experience to show for my efforts.

The prevailing wisdom among my faculty at the time was, "If you can pass the CPA exam, you will find a job." As a result, I changed my major from finance to accounting and obtained a bachelor of science degree within three and a half years in May 1995 with the highest honors (summa cum laude) by taking summer classes. I didn't love accounting, but it was a means to an end and part of my deliberate plan at a time when I had very few resources at my disposal. I ended up graduating in a stronger position than many of the other students, especially foreign students. Many of them had to go back to their country of origin. I prevailed by being adaptable. I got a job as a cost accountant at the West Publishing Company (now Thomson Reuters), which set me on a successful career trajectory, which I will explore more in the next chapter.

Final Thoughts

I use the word "dream" many times in this book. I talk about daring to dream and achieving the American dream. For those of you who grew up in America, this might sound like an overused concept, but for a poor immigrant, it still holds immense power and possibility.

When I left the Bank of China without a college place or even a passport, some people thought that was reckless, but for me at that time, I knew that three years at the bank was enough. I was ready for a new challenge, and when none could be found in China, I found a way to manifest it elsewhere by relying on my own character, my guiding principles, the help of others, and holding fast to my dreams even when those around me tried to tell me I was foolish for having them.

Today, therefore, my advice to others always starts with daring to dream. When setting out on a path to success, the most important question to ask is "What are my dreams?"

To achieve success make sure you continue to dream big. Look back and look ahead. Reflect on the past twenty years, and dream about the next twenty. Write down what you want to achieve over the next year and next three years. You never know whom you will meet or where your dreams will lead.

The next question to ask is "What are the roadblocks for me at this time, or what is holding me back?"

It's important to talk about the challenges and obstacles you need to overcome, but it's also important to dive a little deeper and examine your own personal assets, your personal strengths and traits. What are those traits on which you can rely? Take some assessment tests, such as the Kolbe, DiSC, or Strengths Finder to identify your skills, natural strengths, and passion. Ask other people what they believe to be your greatest strength. When I took the Kolbe test in

2003, I found I had a high score of 8 in the Quick Start category, which means that when dealing with risk and uncertainty, I am built to start new projects and constantly have new ideas to implement and experiment with.

Knowing your strengths helps you play to them on your path to financial independence.

The next chapter explores my career trajectory after college, one that led me to setting up my own firm despite the attempts of other people to hold me back. The seven guiding principles and the lessons I learned on my path will be further explored so that you can apply them to the presentation of wealth management knowledge and advice in subsequent chapters. By the end of this book, you will see that if I could come here with $800 and make it, then you can own your future too.

CHAPTER 2

Adapting in America

Quite often your best-laid plans end up taking an unexpected turn, but these turns can be a door opening to a new opportunity. Even when all options aren't known ahead of time, being prepared and being adaptable to change allows you to capitalize on opportunities as they arise. This might sound confusing—how can you prepare for an opportunity that hasn't presented itself? It's not as strange as it sounds. The key to success for me, and for anyone seeking success, is to adhere to the principles outlined in chapter 1. From following those principles, I learned that devising, assessing, and revising goals can bring an unanticipated level of success.

Echoes of Growth

Adhering to the principles of adaptability and meticulous planning in college paid off upon graduation when the West Publishing Company sponsored me for an H-1B visa for specialty workers and offered me a job doing cost accounting for their legal books. This involved analyzing costs (writers' fees, paper, printing, and marketing), comparing those to similar books in the market, and determining pricing. From this, I could project profit margins based on different variables and make pricing recommendations to my manager, Carol. It was a good first job for a new college graduate. I was a young female Asian, and even a little self-conscious about my accent, but Carol helped me learn the technology and adapt to working in a professional setting.

My conscientiousness and adaptability paid off, and I soon became very proficient in cost analysis. In 1996, I passed the Certified Public Accountant (CPA) exam. However, in less than two years, I had learned everything I could in that job. I had achieved and exceeded the opportunity that had been presented to me and quickly reached the limit of my trajectory. Since West was a publishing company, not an accounting firm, it could not move me closer to my goal of getting a CPA license and putting the letters CPA after my name. Once I learned that the state of Minnesota required a minimum two years of public accounting experience to get a CPA license, my next thought was, "Okay, now where do I get that?"

I had learned on my path from China to America that when a situation seems limiting or limited, it's important to dare to dream and then adapt to manifest that dream. It's important to identify new goals, acquire additional education, and create the opportunities to realize those dreams so that you can own your future in terms of both your lifestyle and financial wealth and health.

It was time to advance, but I had visa restrictions to consider. I would not only have to find a job, but I would have to find a job with a company that would sponsor me for an H-1B work visa.

Next Steps

Becoming a licensed CPA was my next goal, and passing the CPA exam in 1996 strengthened my position to gain permanent US residency. When I first came to the United States, I thought about working in Hong Kong after graduation and after gaining some work experience, but having lived in Minnesota for three years, I knew I wanted to stay in the United States. To do this, I had to advance to the next phase of my career by laying the groundwork for a new opportunity into which I could grow.

When opportunities haven't yet manifested, adaptability and planning can hasten their arrival. In my case, the obvious plan started with networking with the largest CPA firms in the world. I applied to two and got offered a job in the Minneapolis office of KPMG, a professional service company and one of the "Big Four" CPA firms (the others are Deloitte, Ernst & Young, and PricewaterhouseCoopers). KPMG were known at the time for offering top students good in-house training, which not only satisfied my ambition but also appealed to my insatiable desire for education and offered me a way to learn new skills and explore new opportunities.

I was offered a choice between auditing and tax services. At first, I opted for auditing the financial statements of major corporations, such as banks and mutual fund companies. There was a lot of travel involved in auditing, which sounded perfect after almost two years in a small cubicle at West. In addition to traveling, I was auditing financial services companies, which was a new area for me, and as with anything unfamiliar to me, it inspired me to learn everything I could related to this line of business. I have always subscribed to the idea that if you find out you're interested in something, don't hesitate to try it.

I have always subscribed to the idea that if you find out you're interested in something, don't hesitate to try it.

Initially, I loved this job because of the travel it afforded, but I spent far too much time on the road and in hotels in the middle of nowhere, disconnected from my friends and with nothing to do after work. Six months later, I reached out to the KPMG partners and networked throughout the firm to find another opening in tax services. I realized that networking was part of the seventh principle which I'd been living: networking allows you benefit from the wisdom of others. I was not only able to make new contacts, but I also learned what different people do, what they like, and what they don't like.

As I mentioned in chapter 1, it's not always possible to know what opportunities are going to arise, but it's still important to live by the principle of meticulous preparation. I prepared by assessing. I looked at my current position and assessed what skills or experience or contacts or certification were needed to get to my next position. In other words, part of the preparation process involves setting goals and laying the groundwork, part comes from daring to dream and following that which captures the imagination and brings joy to the morning, and part comes from looking around to see who has the wisdom and experience to help.

Learning to network as I did was critical to my success and to how I built my business later. I expanded my network to people outside the company. I discovered professional organizations and joined the Financial Planning Association and the Minnesota Society of CPAs. I have actively volunteered for both organizations. By networking in this way, I learned that within tax services, there were tax specializations, one of which was personal financial planning. There were about twenty people in that KPMG personal financial planning group doing tax planning and personal financial planning for high-income corporate executives of *Fortune* 500 companies and wealthy families. It was a new area in financial services in the midnineties, and KPMG started to offer more financial planning services to existing tax services clients. I brushed up my résumé and scheduled an interview.

Nine months and numerous new skills later, I was able to trade in my isolated hotel life for a cubicle on the forty-second floor of a downtown Minneapolis skyscraper and a job as a tax specialist in the new KPMG personal financial planning group. Life had become much more interesting.

Adapting for Success

In the midnineties, personal financial planning included helping executives decide when to exercise stock options and informing them of the tax consequences of exercising an option at a given price. We helped them prepare tax returns, made dealing with taxes as painless as possible, and advised them on how to transfer wealth to the next generation. I came to love this financial planning aspect of the job far more than tax return preparation itself, but regulatory restrictions prohibited CPA firms from managing investments. This meant that if I wanted to focus more on wealth management, I would have to pivot again.

From Setback to Opportunity

In December 2000, I leapt into the role of financial advisor. I started working for RSM McGladrey, which was related to McGladrey and

Pullen (now RSM US LLP), an audit, tax, and consulting firm, and the fifth largest accounting firm in the United States. RSM had just set up a wealth management services division and offered me a job as a financial advisor with the company, which I accepted. After one week of study, I sat and passed the FINRA Series 7 General Securities exam, which is the most common license for a financial advisor/planner. It allowed me to recommend individual stocks, bonds, and mutual funds to clients to implement their investment plans. My boss was the first financial advisor hired in downtown Minneapolis, which made this an entirely new venture and learning experience and a brand-new service in which we set up accounts from scratch.

Unfortunately, we faced a major challenge, which I had to turn to my advantage. While financial advisors in other companies had enjoyed part of the bull market in the nineties, I was starting out when the stock market was in decline. This meant I had to learn very quickly how to gain prospective clients' trust. I had to learn how to coach them through a difficult time. To do this well, I had started the part-time online courses in the CERTIFIED FINANCIAL PLANNER (CFP®) program from the College for Financial Planning in Denver, Colorado, in 1999. After a two-day certification exam and a six-week wait for results, I finally became a CFP® practitioner, just before my thirtieth birthday.

An interesting aspect of financial planning turned out to be the need to offer far more emotional and behavioral coaching than I had done as a CPA. I had to learn to read clients' minds because often what was left unsaid was more important than what was said. I'll talk about this more in chapter 4 on overcoming behavioral biases.

A key factor in landing my first major account was effective networking. I got to know my colleagues, especially those who prepared tax returns, and as a CPA, I was able to speak to them in their language. This built trust and respect for my understanding and expertise, in addition to having certification in financial planning and the experience gained in financial planning and tax return preparation while at KPMG. All I had done at RSM was remove the tax return preparation and add investment management. I had attended many conferences, networked with and learned from many experienced individuals, and had done a considerable amount of reading on behavioral finance and counseling, which were important in this field. My commitment and diligence earned my colleagues' trust, so I offered them financial planning services and managed amounts of $200,000 to $700,000 on their behalf.

Laying the groundwork in advance by gaining the trust of colleagues offered opportunities to gain experience on smaller accounts. This paid off a short time later when one of them referred to me a young widow who was an existing client of RSM's tax services. She had just inherited $1.8 million, and my colleague thought she would be well served by a female financial planner.

From the outset, I wanted to add value to this new client relationship. I quickly learned her goals and her fears and presented a plan to address short-term cash flow needs and, as she was still young, her long-term growth objective.

It was important to show her that she didn't need to do it alone and that there was a process laid out by the CFP®'s Standards of Professional Conduct to follow, which we'll look at in more detail in chapter 3. As a result of developing this relationship first, she grew confident in my ability to manage her money wisely. After my first presentation, I was not only able to open an account with a check for $1.8 million, but I also had developed a new strength: the ability to combine tax expertise with investment management skills, which is a rare combination in the financial services sector. Working with the widow and seeing myself grow personally and professionally made me more certain that I had chosen the right profession.

Finding Your Sweet Spot

There is always a period of exploration and experimentation in any job. There is always a period where you feel underqualified, but you have to dare to dream, and you have to dare to try. Then, when you find your sweet spot, that area that is most rewarding for you and where your skills and qualities are a perfect fit, it's time to get focused.

I had been experimenting in each job and each role I filled. Each time I assessed, pivoted, and changed tracks. I found new strengths in the combination of different qualities, such as being analytical and detail oriented but also being able to relate to people, which can be rare in the financial services world where so many people are merely trained to sell products and get commissions.

During the first year, when someone said, "Echo, you are not like a typical CPA. You don't fit that CPA stereotype. You are not just a bean counter behind the scenes," I knew this was my sweet spot. I enjoyed simplifying wealth management for people so that they could take control of their lives.

Although I had not been aware of the existence of the new area of personal financial planning for long, when the opportunity arose, I could grasp it due to the cumulative effect of the education I had acquired, the wisdom and networking from which I had benefited, daring to dream and daring to try, and playing to my strengths and passion. In other words, from constantly assessing and laying groundwork in the areas in which I was most interested, the path became clear.

Rejecting Limitations

I became very successful at managing people's wealth at RSM after opening that $1.8 million account, which was why my pivotal decision to leave RSM and set up my own company surprised many people. However, as with most pivotal decision points in my life, I discovered that the groundwork had been laid to allow me to extricate myself from limitation and grasp a new opportunity.

In 2002, my boss, with whom I'd worked well, was promoted to regional director, and my new boss, who was hired from the outside, for whatever reason, was not curious about me or my passion or potential. He hired a white male advisor also from the outside, whom I had to train on the system I had created for the firm. I soon learned that he had been hired at a manager-level pay grade and was earning more than me. Given that I had put all the work into creating the system and building the group at RSM, I should have been considered first for promotion.

My initial upset became a determination to move forward, if not within RSM, then elsewhere. I knew I had to get out from under the glass ceiling that limited women, and even more so, a female Asian immigrant. I've encountered discriminatory pay scales multiple times in my career. I knew that, in a huge company like RSM, I would not be able to change that. I needed a scenario that would offer equal opportunity and equal pay. As with the Bank of China years before, I decided to quit.

My family was concerned about me giving up a private office with windows facing the IDS building in downtown Minneapolis, along with a large company's benefits including health insurance and the matching contributions to the 401(k) plan, but I was not prepared to sit there and be victim to unfair practices or inequality. I refused to fall victim to others' limitations.

I was not prepared to sit there and be victim to unfair practices or inequality. I refused to fall victim to others' limitations.

In March 2003, I started working as a solo financial advisor with the independent brokerage firm, LPL Financial (formerly Linsco Private Ledger). I managed close to $20 million in less than three years by networking with CPAs and other professionals. In June 2005, after my daughter, Nina, was born, I merged with another firm called The Advocate Group. I became a minority owner, which freed up more time to be with Nina. After nine years there, focusing on serving corporate executives with *Fortune* 500 companies and enhancing its financial planning processes and tools, I decided to leave and set up Echo Wealth Management as a registered investment advisor (RIA) in February 2015, which would embody my planning and investment philosophy and create a culture with better gender equity. This time, my family—knowing that I had built a network of many high-net-worth clients—was very supportive of my decision.

Few women do my job. This may be because they do not see the profession as a viable option or do not see themselves in it. About twenty years ago, 23 percent of CFP® professionals were women. Today, that number hasn't changed,[4] despite the fact that the number of women getting college degrees has increased dramatically over the last twenty to thirty years. I believe this is due to misconceptions about the nature of the financial planning profession. Many people see it as sales in the traditional sense of selling products to get commissions, and women tend to steer clear of selling. Women don't realize that the skills that make someone succeed as a financial

---

4 Kerry Hannon, "Where Are All The Female Financial Advisers?" *Forbes* (May 8, 2014). Available at https://www.forbes.com/sites/nextavenue/2014/05/08/where-are-all-the-female-financial-advisers/#4880e9972d81.

planner include solid financial training, good communications, and relationship building. Gender discrimination remains an issue—not feeling welcome and getting paid much less than men with the same experience, revenue production, and ownership. Unfortunately, all of this means that there are many women who want female financial advisors but find there aren't enough to serve the market.

The obvious way for me to get around gender inequality was to set up my own company. I knew I had to go out there, clear the path for myself, and do this on my own. Setting up my own firm—Echo Wealth Management—was the way I could truly change the status quo.

Final Thoughts

During this midstage of my career, I was always gaining new skills, trying different tasks, and making adjustments based on my passion and interests. At each stage, I learned something that I could take forward that was in line with my passion and interests. One of these lessons was that adaptability is a key ingredient when it comes to maximizing success so that you can own your future.

It's important to look at your willingness to adapt. Ask yourself: Are you adapting to fit into your environment instead of respecting your own passion and interests? As you can see from my story, at the end of the day, you need to go out and get a job that you love to be successful. If you hate your job today, you need to assess what is wrong with it and what you like about it, and use that to find your next job.

Ask yourself if you are learning new skills in your current job while being open-minded about finding better opportunities. Skills are often transferable between jobs; I was able to transfer skills from tax accounting to wealth management. Constantly assess what you can do to develop skills that you can leverage later.

Never become complacent. You can't jump without the preparation and education that will make you stand out. Always think about what would make you stand out so that you can get to the next place where you are more passionate about your job.

Adaptability allows you maximize your experience on any job. It allows you think in terms of exploration of opportunities and an expansion of your skill set. Never be complacent with the skill set you have because you never know when an opportunity will arise that demand your particular combination of qualities. It allows you to be prepared so that you can mitigate risks when it comes to actually making a leap when an opportunity arises.

It's always important to expand your range of skills and your network. Therefore, ask yourself what you can do today that will, in terms of networking or education, help you identify your strengths and passions to position yourself where you want to be. If you can play to your strengths, you'll find yourself in a position that speaks to your passion. Once you are great at something, you'll naturally succeed.

If you are in an ideal job where you are playing to your strengths and showing excellence in performance, you are likely maximizing your pay increases and promotional opportunities. It's now time to increase and manage the wealth you are accumulating. In the next chapters, I'll present a process for wealth management to give you the information you need to take the necessary steps to financial success and from there to owning your future.

CHAPTER 3

Wealth Management Can Be Complicated (But Doesn't Have to Be)

Remember how simple things were when you were a kid? Life was good. Everything you owned could fit into a box. All your worldly possessions were in one safe place, which made you feel secure. Then, as time passed, you collected more things and more boxes, and life became less simple. Like many people, you may have suddenly noticed that life had gotten more and more complicated, and you'd arrived at a point in time where you didn't know where everything was or what everything was worth. Then you noticed that acquiring assets and new accounts has led to a complex account management and tax treatment. You knew you needed to get involved in wealth management, but it

The bottom line is this: if you have accumulated substantial assets, you need a wealth management service, and the more assets you acquire, the more complicated management becomes.

sounded so complicated, you didn't know where to start.

The bottom line is this: if you have accumulated substantial assets, you need a wealth management service, and the more assets you acquire, the more complicated management becomes. Life circumstances and career advances change wealth management needs. For example, someone who gets promoted to be an officer of a *Fortune* 500 company may suddenly find themselves with restrictive stock awards, performance shares, nonqualified stock options, a pension, a 401(k) plan, and a deferred compensation plan as part of their compensation package. Chances are, they will lose track of where everything is and what everything is worth.

Don't despair! Wealth management can be complicated, but it doesn't have to be. In this chapter, we'll explore how to think about wealth management to avoid overwhelm. The focus here is not on explaining how to manage taxes or investment funds and strategies— we will look at that in later chapters on investment management, estate planning, tax strategies, and other aspects of a financial plan that need to be managed. In this chapter, we'll simply demystify the idea of wealth management so that you can better understand how to do this yourself or how to talk to a wealth manager should you opt to engage a professional advisor/planner.

FOUR COMMON PROBLEMS

The most common issue I encounter when people come to me for help is that they have never organized their assets in such a way that they can answer the question "What is your net worth?" Without knowing their net worth, they can't achieve their goals, particularly retirement goals. They rarely know how much they need when they retire, which translates into not knowing when they can retire. In other words, many people don't know where they are right now or what they need to get to where they want to go.

A second issue is emotional investing. Individual investors in particular are more likely to make quick and emotional decisions. They often make the wrong decisions during market downturns. They panic when the market drops and sell, which means they sell low, then sit the market out and wait until it takes an upturn to get back in, which means they are buying high. We'll look at this more in chapter 4 when we talk about behavioral finance and cognitive biases.

The third mistake many people make is too infrequently reviewing their insurance needs and coverage, particularly long-term disability insurance. An executive with earning power or someone who earns $600,000 a year, for example, and has a stay-at-home spouse and three children in private school, will have a financial plan that relies on their ability to earn income. If they become disabled, their plan won't work. Many people, those in their forties in particular, fail to take the time or develop the expertise (or consult an expert as part of a team) to correctly analyze their insurance needs. As a result, they tend to underinsure in terms of disability insurance. Some breadwinners don't have enough life insurance coverage to replace their earned income if they die before retirement.

Another common issue I encounter is that of people who, over the years, accumulate accounts in different places end up with fifteen or more statements coming in every month. Not only does this incur a lot of fees, it makes determining net worth even more complicated. It is almost impossible to monitor asset allocation closely to execute investment strategies timely. This was the case with Violet,[5] a successful businesswoman who came to me in desperate need of wealth management.

Violet's Story

Violet is a fifty-year-old VP of marketing at a large, publicly traded company. She came just after she lost her job with an idea to begin consulting rather than seeking new employment. She needed to know if she could afford to make this decision based on her accumulated assets. She had received free financial advice from her godfather for many years before he retired. She had a highly concentrated position in her former employer's stock, a 401(k) plan with the company, and investments in fifteen mutual funds that she had opened directly with different fund companies. She also had two 401(k) accounts from old employers with balances that were never transferred.

Since her mutual funds were not held by one custodian/brokerage firm, they could not be easily monitored. As a result, she got quarterly statements from each company, so struggled to know her net worth. She was also paying a lot in fees and expenses. Most of her retirement money was in a 401(k) plan with the company she had just left along with a small IRA that she had put money into many years earlier. She had an old estate plan that hadn't been updated. She had a tax accountant who did her tax returns, but he was not working with her financial advisor. She had no trusted advisor monitoring all her

5 People's real names have been changed throughout.

investments and their performance in terms of risk and reward. Her advisor had simply advised her to invest $50,000–$100,000 based on the funds having a good record without taking her risk profile and her cash flow plan into account. She was working with a number of individuals but didn't have a team, so there was no central organization. There was no one to tell her how or where to adjust. Her portfolio was scattered due to the piecemeal advice she had received over the years.

Violet's situation is not uncommon. Many people get into this position by starting out in her career with very little money and an investment only in a 401(k). As their career advances, they get promoted and have more money to invest but don't have the time or interest to do it with any sort of educated or informed decisions or meticulous planning. They don't know their net worth and haven't done a financial plan to determine whether their current retirement savings are enough to retire at a given age.

The loss of her corporate job was a major transition in Violet's life. She wanted to set herself up as an independent consultant rather than look for another corporate job, and she came to us wondering if she had enough assets to pursue this goal without making major changes to her lifestyle. She was at a critical decision point. She had a goal but didn't have the information, knowledge, and expertise she needed to make an informed decision. She needed expert help to do this planning.

Violet had a clear trigger point. Others simply come to see us because they have gotten to a point where they are tired of the financial chaos caused by a badly managed or haphazard portfolio and realize they desperately need a financial plan.

The Seven-Step Financial Planning Process

The CFP® Standards of Professional Conduct define financial planning as "the process of determining whether and how an individual can meet life goals through the proper management of financial resources. Financial planning integrates the financial planning process with the financial planning subject areas."

After a client relationship is established and defined by signing a financial planning agreement, every CFP® practitioner must follow the seven-step financial planning process defined by the CFP® Standards of Professional Conduct. This process starts with the first step during a discovery meeting.

1. Understand the personal and financial circumstances.

2. Identify and select goals.

3. Analyze current course of action and potential alternative course of action.

4. Develop recommendations.

5. Present recommendations.

6. Implement recommendations.

7. Monitor and update progress.

It doesn't matter if a client comes into us with $10 million or $500,000, we follow the same financial planning process. It's important that clients understand the CFP® designation; it not only means that we have undergone training and education in wealth management, but also that we have to act in accordance with CFP® Board's fiduciary duty and apply the Practice Standards when providing financial planning service.

The Discovery Meeting

During our initial discovery meeting with a new client, we ask many questions such as "What is your earliest money memory?" "How do you discuss and manage finances with your spouse?" "What activities would you like to do now if you just learned that you have one year to live?" "What does financial independence look like for you?" in order to learn about their values and their priorities. After we have gathered data about their net worth, we dive into understanding their lifestyle. We enter all their information into my wealth management tool, Echo Dashboard, which I'll explore more in the next section. When creating an Echo Dashboard for each client, we include all their accounts, which paints a picture of their financial situation including income and living expenses.

Living expenses differ from individual to individual, depending on their lifestyle. This makes lifestyle a key factor in wealth management by using the correct living expenses to calculate the capital clients need to achieve to retire. Analyzing credit card statements can capture spending patterns, especially if the client uses them a lot. We then look at the checking and savings account balances and debts, including mortgage accounts.

Most people seem to find spending patterns the most tedious part. They don't want to bother with the trouble of tracking their expenses. Regardless what tools you use to create a budget and track expenses, doing this exercise of categorizing expenses into two major categories: essential expenses and discretionary expenses. Then, creating subcategories will provide clarity on how you earn income and how you spend money. After three months of tracking every expense, you will have much better sense of which areas you can improve to increase savings.

In my meeting with Violet, my next question was where she wanted to go and when. From there we could explore what roadblocks and challenges she faced, which allowed me to identify where she needed help. She didn't have an issue with children or factors such as college planning. Other clients can be juggling family, raising children, and holding down demanding jobs that leave little time to look at an investment statement, never mind research smart investments. Even if a client is clear about their goals and their strengths, they are likely not a "do-it-yourselfer." In fact, most successful and intelligent clients who come to me don't want to have to put in more than ten or twenty hours a year into their wealth management.

I regularly write about wealth management issues in my blog so that clients can learn about money along the way. The result is that when I make a recommendation, they understand to some degree. For example, they'll remember reading about the special triple tax benefits of a health savings account (HSA). The rest of their time, however, should be focused on their own talents and strengths and to putting ten or twenty hours into what they do best rather than wrestling with their own limitations.

Think about it—you don't paint your house; you hire that out. It's not that you don't know how to paint; it's that if you are earning $300,000 a year in a job that involves equity compensation, such as stock options, it's probably not worth your time to try to deal with painting your house. It's the same with wealth management, except the financial markets and tax laws change constantly. It's probably not worth your time to try to deal with it on your own, especially if you don't know how to maximize various benefits offered by your employer.

The next question asked in Violet's discovery meeting, as in all discovery meetings with new clients, was designed to give me an understanding of her money story. I asked her what were the best and worst financial decisions she ever made. A person's answer to this offers great insights into their choices and how they learn lessons as a result of those choices. This offers a good understanding of who they are and how they'll make decisions in the future. The better I understand how a client reacts, the better prepared I am to guide them along the way.

For example, I often ask people about their health, their job satisfaction, their career path, and where they think they're going. I ask if they would be willing to delay retirement or reduce living expenses if the financial planning projection for the target retirement date does not look feasible. I also want to know their family longevity history and find out how people feel about longevity. I ask what they think they will do after retirement, because an early retiree may live thirty more years, and if that happens, they'll need to find a passion in order to be engaged and stay healthy.

The goal of a discovery is to understand the client in order to propose a plan that offers them choices; for example, someone can look at scenarios that offer them choices between cutting back on expenses and early retirement or maintaining their current lifestyle but delaying retirement. Using the Echo Dashboard, we can show them the permutations of how any given decision can be made to change these elements as their lifestyle and preferences change over time. In other words, we build not just a current financial picture, but the picture of an entire life.

In the first year with new clients, we normally have four office or screen-share meetings (ninety minutes each) with the advisor to go through the entire financial planning process in the first three months. Then we put the plan into action to implement agreed-upon strategies that may include changing investments, buying more insurance, revising their estate plan, and visiting a tax CPA for tax planning. The second year and beyond, most clients visit us every six months to review and adjust their financial plans if they have finished implementing our recommendations in the first twelve months and use Echo Dashboard to monitor their goals.

Echo Dashboard

The Echo Dashboard is a powerful tool that is developed and supported by eMoney Advisor. We began using it in 2005. Today, we exploit all of its utility to aggregate a client's accounts' balances, including the accounts that we do not proactively manage, such as 401(k) plan and checking and savings accounts. For clients with equity compensation, we manually enter current and projected stock options and restricted stock awards to track every grant, and the values are updated daily automatically based on the stock price. We can project the stock value and earned income from the equity plans based on the annual growth rate assumption (5 or 6 percent) and calculate tax impacts every year based on current tax laws in all fifty states.

On a day-to-day basis, setting a client up with Echo Dashboard allows them, and us, to see everything they own in a private and secure location where all their data is consolidated into one clear financial picture. This makes getting organized simple. It shows current and projected income, net worth, and expenses year-by-year to age ninety-five based on some key assumptions, including date of retirement, inflation, and target rate of return.

Each night, the Echo Dashboard pulls the balances and the security positions from the institutions where the client has accounts. The balances are recalculated to keep the client up to date as their account values change. Automatic alerts track changes in the accounts, so if a problem or opportunity arises, we'll know about it. Then, to help the client stay on track, we help them create a monthly budget to understand their spending habits and monitor their progress. They can see their bottom line at any time on any device. Their Echo Dashboard even has a digital vault where they can safely store their important personal documents, photos, and videos.

I cannot recommend highly enough that you find a tool like the Echo Dashboard to consolidate and track all of your accounts and then project your future cash flow and net worth over time.

In short, the Echo Dashboard gives clients the tools to connect with everything they own so they know what everything is worth. No matter where a person is or what they're doing, those who know what they have fare better than those who don't. I cannot recommend highly enough that you find a tool like the Echo Dashboard to consolidate and track all of your accounts and then project your future cash flow and net worth over time.

In Violet's situation, it didn't matter that she had twenty accounts because all the information was consolidated into her net worth statement, including her home and other properties. Her mortgage loan and the interest were calculated and included. The Echo Dashboard showed her projected detailed inflows and outflows, including lifestyle expenses and taxes, using yesterday's account values until she turned ninety-five.

After we presented specific recommendations on savings and investment strategies by showing the projections on the Echo Dashboard, and once we got her approval to go ahead, we began to manage her money with discretionary trading authorizations. We chose two qualified custodians to open accounts in clients' names: TD

Ameritrade and Charles Schwab. We do not take custody of clients' assets. In Violet's case, she took our recommendation to consolidate into only three accounts (IRA, Roth IRA, and trust accounts) at TD Ameritrade by transferring money from various fund companies and old 401(k) plans. The consolidation of her funds with TD Ameritrade meant not only could she see everything in one place and avoid paying hidden fees, but she also could see that her customized portfolio was designed around her risk tolerance and time horizon. She reduced the number of tax forms during tax seasons, and she was also happy about not receiving paper statements.

Exploring Options

With all clients, making their data available in their dashboard account any time means we are in a position to run "what if" scenarios. These scenarios are key to establishing a proper wealth management plan. This process makes it very easy to see how outlays and savings or other actions over the long term affect a wealth profile. Since the dashboard projects a client's profile up to the age of ninety-five, running scenarios makes it possible to view the potential impact of a decision not just today but throughout the client's lifetime.

Violet had a clear goal, so we devised different plans for different scenarios to give her the information she needed. In order to set up a consulting business, she needed to know, for example, whether she needed to jump into the next job that came along or could rather take eighteen months to lay the groundwork that could lead to her consulting business.

Our plan also told her how much money she could spend and still reach her goals. In her case, she learned that she could continue as a consultant working part time without needing to return to the corporate world if she earned $80,000 a year for the next five years. This was a relief for her. From this planning, she knew that if an extremely attractive job came her way, she could take it because she wanted it, not because she needed it. This meant she also had the choice to continue as a consultant while maintaining her current lifestyle and growth goals so that she could retire on her target date.

The Echo Dashboard shows all of our clients the impact of their decisions on cash flow, tax planning, estate planning, college funding, and insurance, as well as the impact a premature death, disability, or long-term care would have on their family members. This allows them to make adjustments in order to have a solid and comprehensive financial plan that protects them and their family into the future.

When Is a Tool Not Just a Tool?

A surgeon with twenty years' experience of an operation procedure will fine-tune his or her technique to get a better outcome despite using the same equipment (a scalpel) as another surgeon. It's the same with money. The procedure needs to be something the client believes in and not merely be a tool throwing out numbers that fit into cookie-cutter financial planning.

By fine-tuning how we use the data from the dashboard, we offer more ways to reach a goal. Not only does the tool allow the client to see their financial picture, it also frees me up from tracking data and allows me to spend an hour listening to money stories instead. This helps me understand how to help people make the decisions they need to make. A competent advisor should utilize updated technologies in order to increase productivity and create better client experiences because clients expect their advisors to be more proactive, and the advice delivered is customized to them while keeping the costs reasonable.

If you are overwhelmed by your financial picture and want to work with an advisor, find an advisor who understands what you value in order to help you prioritize your goals and progress, identify gaps in your plan, and recommend alternative actions. Your advisor needs to be focused on you, understand your situation, speak to you in a language you understand, allay your fears about investing, and offer you demonstrable scenarios and outcomes. You have various goals and competing resources, so make sure you work with someone who uses a robust tool that can help you see clearly when you need money, how much you need, and what you need to do to reach your goals.

Final Thoughts

When it comes to thinking about wealth management, it's important to ask yourself six questions:

1. Do you know your net worth?

2. Do you have clear goals?

3. Are you daring to dream?

4. Do you know your annual living expenses?

5. Have you been saving money systematically for your retirement goals?

6. Do you have a management system in place so that you are not spending too much time on wealth management that might be better served elsewhere, particularly if wealth management isn't your strength?

Even if you're not working with a wealth manager, understand the basic framework of financial planning and how you can benefit from it. Figure out your net worth, how much you spend, how much you need to save in your 401(k) or IRA, write down your goals, and continually review to assess how well you're doing. Remember, you can start your own financial planning from wherever you are. You don't have to wait until a day when you have a substantial amount of money. If you create healthy money habits by starting to plan now, even with a small amount money, you will get to your goal a lot faster.

Violet's goal is shared by many people. She had a dream and then set her goals to achieve this dream; she needed to get organized, acquire some basic education, be adaptable, and build a team to become financially independent. We'll look at the concept of financial independence in chapter 5, but first, let's look at common behavioral biases that can sabotage your financial plan.

CHAPTER 4

Overcoming Behavioral Biases

A few years ago, Mrs. Burgundy came to me to manage her portfolio, which was composed a lot of Ecolab stock that she had received over the years from her father, who had worked there for many years, and her own employer's stock in her 401(k) plan that she hadn't touched for over twenty years. The cost basis of Ecolab stock was very low. These two stocks accounted for 85 percent of her portfolio. Despite a conservative risk tolerance, she insisted on holding onto this precarious, non-diversified portfolio because both stocks had performed well over the years. She never explored the downside should Ecolab stock collapse. In other words, her decision was inconsistent with her risk profile and investment goals. Mrs. Burgundy had an emotional bias known as status quo bias.

For many years, economists believed that investors considered all available information and acted in a rational and wealth-maximizing manner when it came to making investment decisions. They believed this made markets efficient. Unfortunately, markets often show anomalies, such as extreme rises or falls in stock prices, which shouldn't happen if investors were rational. This led behavioral economists, such as Richard Thaler of the University of Chicago, to investigate the cause. Thaler noticed that incongruities or biases in human behavior were behind the problem.[6] It turned out that people were making irrational decisions based on a number of different biases, largely emotional, which caused them to make investment mistakes that were not in their own best interest.

In general, behavioral biases fall into one of two categories: cognitive biases and emotional biases. Each comes with its own particular set of drawbacks. Cognitive errors stem from basic statistical, information-processing, or memory errors; cognitive errors may be considered the result of faulty reasoning. Emotional biases stem from impulse or intuition; emotional biases may be considered to result from reasoning influenced by feelings. Both types of bias lead us to make decisions that are very different from the type of rational decisions finance has traditionally assumed people make.[7]

Today, in the fields of psychology and economics, it's largely accepted that people are wired with natural biases that adversely affect their self-interest. This means that being a good investor is not just a matter of being informed; it also means you need to understand what's motivating your behavior.

The first step to wealth management success is to be aware that these biases exist, challenge yourself to see if you are guilty of

6 The Nobel Prize, "Press release: The Prize in Economic Sciences 2017," (October 9, 2017). Available at https://www.nobelprize.org/prizes/economic-sciences/2017/press-release/.

7 Michael M. Pompian. *Behavioral Finance and Wealth Management: How to Build Investment Strategies.* New York: John Wiley & Sons, 2011.

one or more of them, and then take actions to overcome them. In this chapter, we'll examine some of the common biases that may be causing you to make suboptimal investment decisions that are affecting your bottom line.

I present five common emotional biases that you will want to be aware of, as well as some advice on how to modify your behavior and adapt to these biases.

Status Quo Bias

I meet many clients who have what's called "status quo bias." Status quo bias is an emotional bias in which people do nothing instead of making a change. People are generally more comfortable keeping things the same than with change and thus do not necessarily look for opportunities where change is beneficial.

In Mrs. Burgundy's case, she was holding a non-diversified portfolio that was at odds with her risk profile. Because she hadn't had any visible problems with her portfolio, she believed her two stocks to be safe stocks, and since she had a fear of making the wrong decision, she preferred to maintain the status quo.

The consequences of this bias are that you could unknowingly maintain portfolios with risk characteristics that are inappropriate for you. You may then fail to explore other opportunities instead by quantifying the risk-reducing and return-enhancing advantages of diversification and proper asset allocation.

Status quo bias can be exceptionally strong and difficult to overcome. In Mrs. Burgundy's case, she overcame it by seeing the scenarios we ran in the Echo Dashboard and some tools. We were able to show her a comparison of the performance of these stocks in a volatile market when these stocks weren't doing well versus a more diversified

People know they need to save for retirement, but they often have difficulty sacrificing present consumption because of a lack of self-control.

portfolio. We quantified downside risk in understandable terms— that is to say, dollar amounts. This showed her how precarious her wealth was and how underperformance of one stock would delay her retirement. In addition to providing some education, it was important to help her adapt by taking some small steps, not selling these two stocks in

a single year. With this insight, she then took our advice to diversify by selling her employer stock inside her 401(k) plan first without any tax impact and then set up target prices to gradually sell Ecolab stock. In addition, she transferred some low-cost-basis Ecolab stock to her donor-advised fund every year to reduce income taxes and avoid paying taxes on the long-term capital gains when the stock was sold inside her donor-advised fund to diversify. Today, her portfolio is more diversified, and she is more comfortable taking some risks because she's had some positive investing experience to challenge her status quo bias and has educated herself about risk and returns trade-offs.

Self-Control Bias

Self-control bias is an emotional bias in which people fail to act in pursuit of their long-term, overarching goals because of a lack of self-discipline. People know they need to save for retirement, but they often have difficulty sacrificing present consumption because of a lack of self-control. The apparent lack of self-control may also be a function of hyperbolic discounting, (i.e., the human tendency to prefer small payoffs now compared to large payoffs in the future) and result in having insufficient savings. Then, realizing that their savings are insufficient, investors often:

- Accept too much risk in their portfolios in an attempt to generate higher returns and put their capital base at risk.

- Cause asset allocation imbalance problems. For example, some investors may prefer income-producing assets in order to have the income to spend. This behavior can be hazardous to long-term wealth because income-producing assets may offer less total return potential, particularly when the income is not invested, which may inhibit a portfolio's ability to maintain spending power after inflation.

To mitigate the negative impact of self-control bias, it's important that you create a financial plan to address retirement savings and have a personal budget. In her 2001 paper "Explaining Why So Many People Do Not Save,"[8] Annamaria Lusardi notes that "saving levels depend significantly on whether a household has planned for retirement." A trusted financial advisor can help you with setting clear and actionable savings goals and then help you stick to them. This plan needs to be in writing so that it can be reviewed regularly. It is advisable to consider ways to save more that don't rely on self-control; for example, automatic savings in your 401(k) plan, increasing savings over time, and increasing savings when you get a raise are all good ways to ensure that you have enough money later. It is also advisable to understand and visualize the impact of compounding. Additional monthly savings of $200 can potentially grow to a substantial number ($200,903 at annualized return of 6 percent) over three decades.

8 Annamaria Lusardi, "Explaining Why So Many People Do Not Save" (2001). Center for Retirement Research at Boston College. Available at https://crr.bc.edu/wp-content/uploads/2001/09/wp_2001-05.pdf.

Remember, failing to plan is planning to fail. Adhering to a saving plan and an appropriate asset allocation strategy are critical to long-term financial success.

Inheritance/Endowment Bias

According to economist Richard Thaler,[9] "The fact that people often demand much more to give up an object than they would be willing to acquire it—is called the endowment effect." Some clients who have an inheritance suffer from an inheritance/endowment bias. This is a common emotional bias in which people may irrationally hold onto securities they already own, particularly inherited investments, either for reasons of loyalty, or in some cases, taxes or transaction costs. This can lead to a failure to sell certain assets and replace them with an appropriate asset allocation for investors' levels of risk tolerance and financial goals because the investor has an emotional attachment to the inherited assets.

This bias also applies to the belief that what an investor already owns is worth more. They are familiar with what they own, and this gives them a perceived sense of security. This was evident in Mrs. Burgundy's need to hold onto her stocks. The endowment bias, closely linked to regret aversion and the status quo bias, often causes us to hold on to securities long after they're no longer relevant to our goals.

Experience helps to fight this. Experienced investors know the law of one price, and you may need help from someone who is sophisticated in dealing with these types of investments.

One way to overcome inheritance bias is to ask yourself, "If an equivalent sum to the value of the investments inherited had been

9 Daniel Kahneman, Jack L. Knetsch, and Richard H. Thaler, "Experimental Tests of the Endowment Effect and the Coase Theorem," *Journal of Political Economy* 98, no. 6 (1990): 1325–1348.

received in cash, how would I invest the cash?" Often, the answer is into a very different investment portfolio than the one inherited. For example, think of the inheritance as a savings account. If someone inherited $1 million in cash in a savings account, they will want to adopt a strategy of investing it in a portfolio with diverse asset classes. However, if this $1 million is in property or stocks, they lose sight of this strategy.

Regret-Aversion Bias

Regret-aversion bias is an emotional bias in which people tend to avoid making decisions that will result in action out of fear that the decision will turn out poorly. I have sat in discovery meetings with some new clients who have been trying to avoid the pain of regret associated with bad decisions.

One consequence of regret-aversion bias is overly conservative investment choices, which are often based on risky investments and losses in the past. This can lead to long-term underperformance and potential failure to reach investment goals. A classic example of this bias is people being reluctant to sell when they should because they fear that the position will increase in value and then they will regret having sold it.

According to Michael Pompian,[10] "regret causes people to challenge past decisions and to question their beliefs," neither of which we as humans tend to enjoy. When the outcomes of the decision are highly visible or accessible, as is the case with stock data, regret becomes even more powerful.

Another consequence of regret-aversion bias is herding behavior. Herding happens when someone finds security in doing

---

10 Michael M. Pompian. *Behavioral Finance and Wealth Management: How to Build Investment Strategies.* New York: John Wiley & Sons, 2011.

what everyone else is doing. If everybody is buying in, he or she will feel safe buying in. If everybody is selling, he or she will feel safer selling. However, buying when everyone is buying is the wrong time to buy because you'll end up buying high. On the flip side, people often sell when a price is falling and they see everyone else selling, which is precisely the wrong time to sell because they'll lose money. This is classic herding behavior; there is a perception that potential emotional pain will be reduced if it's shared with the crowd.

To identify regret aversion, consider cataloging how you felt after making investment decisions and looking at when you were most likely to regret them? If you start to spot a trend, that will give you insights to how to act in the future. Other important tips for dealing with this bias include setting price targets to take the emotion out of the buy or sell decision as well as making sure that each decision is well researched and consistent with your asset allocation strategy and long-term goals. Remember that the market goes in cycles; losses happen as well as gains. This will help you to see the benefits of having conservative as well as risky assets in your portfolio over the long term.

Overconfidence Bias

Overconfidence bias occurs when clients demonstrate unwarranted faith in their own intuitive reasoning, judgments, and/or cognitive abilities. It is a cognitive bias that may result from overestimating knowledge, abilities, and access to information. This may be intensified when combined with self-attribution bias, which occurs when they take credit for successes and assign responsibility for failures. They may rely on faulty reasoning, a "gut feeling" and emotional factors, such as hope, all of which leads to prediction overconfidence and certainty overconfidence.

I have seen the consequences of overconfidence bias when clients underestimate risks and overestimate expected returns, hold poorly diversified portfolios, trade excessively, and experience lower returns than those of the market.

To challenge potential overconfidence bias, make sure you don't study individual investments in isolation, and make sure to keep a comparative analysis perspective. This can help keep your own assessments realistic. Think of the investment as being part of a set of comparisons, and then ground your analysis in the average risk and return for that set. In addition, review your trading records, identify the winners and losers, and calculate portfolio performance over at least two years. A conscious review process will give you a realistic picture of your investment decisions. Look for patterns or common mistakes you are making, then brainstorming a rule (e.g., "I will do X in the future" or "I will not do Y in the future").

Now that you know the common emotional biases and the ways to mitigate the negative consequences, I will discuss the common cognitive biases next.

Representativeness Bias

When faced with uncertainty, we have seen some clients relying on a mental shortcut known as representativeness bias. Representativeness bias is a belief perseverance bias in which people tend to classify uncertain information based on past experiences. We tend to estimate the likelihood of an outcome or return by comparing it to an existing base point that already exists in our minds. For example, an investor could categorize Company ABC as a "growth stock" as a result of finding information about ABC that is consistent with the investor's beliefs, but then neglect to adequately account for the base rate.

They might focus more heavily on recent information, putting more weight on high returns during a one-, two-, or three-year period, rather than focusing on the original or base rate of the investment or the base probability of such a return occurring.

Another way investors fall into representative bias is through sample-size neglect, often called the law of small numbers. This is an erroneous belief in probability, whereby investors mistakenly believe that a small sample is representative of or similar in characteristics to the population. For example, investors tend to buy into a fund immediately following rapid price appreciation.[11] They seem to categorize the funds as good investments based on this recent information. However, these increases tend to precede a subsequent decline in the fund's performance. Then, when prices fall, investors sell this fund and search for the next hot fund. Studies[12] of investor behavior by DALBAR, show that this bias has led to average equity investors earning an annualized return of just 3.88 percent—underperforming the S&P 500 Index, which earned 5.62 percent in the past twenty years. During the same period, average fixed-income investors only earned an annualized return of 0.22 percent—underperforming the Bloomberg Barclay US Aggregate Bond Index, which earned 4.55 percent.

To counteract the effects of the representativeness bias when considering returns, we use what has become known as the asset class returns chart,[13] which shows that asset class returns are highly variable.

---

11 DALBAR, "Quantitative Analysis of Investor Behavior" (n.d.). Available at https://www.dalbar.com/QAIB/Index.

12 Capital Group, *DALBAR Investing Study* (2019). Available at https://www.american-funds.com/advisor/pdf/shareholder/ingefl-050_dalbar.pdf.

13 J.P. Morgan Asset Management, "Guide to the Markets" (December 31, 2018). Available at https://am.jpmorgan.com/us/en/asset-management/gim/adv/insights/guide-to-the-markets/viewer.

Asset class returns — GTM – U.S. | 60

	2004	2005	2006	2007	2008	2009	2010	2011	2012	2013	2014	2015	2016	2017	2018	2004 - 2018 Ann.	2004 - 2018 Vol.
1	REITs 31.6%	EM Equity 34.5%	REITs 35.1%	EM Equity 39.8%	Fixed Income 5.2%	EM Equity 79.0%	REITs 27.9%	REITs 8.3%	REITs 19.7%	Small Cap 38.8%	REITs 28.0%	REITs 2.8%	Small Cap 21.3%	EM Equity 37.8%	Cash 1.8%	REITs 8.5%	REITs 22.4%
2	EM Equity 26.0%	Comdty. 21.4%	EM Equity 32.6%	Comdty. 16.2%	Cash 1.8%	High Yield 59.4%	Small Cap 26.9%	Fixed Income 7.8%	High Yield 19.6%	Large Cap 32.4%	Large Cap 13.7%	Large Cap 1.4%	High Yield 14.3%	DM Equity 25.6%	Fixed Income 0.0%	EM Equity 8.3%	EM Equity 22.1%
3	DM Equity 20.7%	DM Equity 14.0%	DM Equity 26.9%	DM Equity 11.6%	Asset Alloc. -25.4%	DM Equity 32.5%	EM Equity 19.2%	High Yield 3.1%	EM Equity 18.6%	DM Equity 23.3%	Fixed Income 6.0%	Fixed Income 0.5%	Large Cap 12.0%	Large Cap 21.8%	REITs -4.0%	Large Cap 7.8%	Small Cap 18.6%
4	Small Cap 18.3%	REITs 12.2%	Small Cap 18.4%	Asset Alloc. 7.1%	High Yield -26.9%	REITs 28.0%	Comdty. 16.8%	Large Cap 2.1%	DM Equity 17.9%	Asset Alloc. 14.9%	Asset Alloc. 5.2%	Cash 0.0%	Comdty. 11.8%	Small Cap 14.6%	High Yield -4.1%	Small Cap 7.5%	Comdty. 18.6%
5	High Yield 13.2%	Asset Alloc. 8.1%	Large Cap 15.8%	Fixed Income 7.0%	Small Cap -33.8%	Small Cap 27.2%	Large Cap 15.1%	Cash 0.1%	Small Cap 16.3%	High Yield 7.3%	Small Cap 4.9%	DM Equity -0.4%	EM Equity 11.6%	Asset Alloc. 14.6%	Large Cap -4.4%	High Yield 7.3%	DM Equity 17.6%
6	Asset Alloc. 12.8%	Large Cap 4.9%	Asset Alloc. 15.3%	Large Cap 5.5%	Large Cap -37.0%	Large Cap 26.5%	High Yield 14.8%	Asset Alloc. -0.7%	Large Cap 16.0%	REITs 2.9%	High Yield 0.0%	Asset Alloc. -2.0%	REITs 8.6%	High Yield 10.4%	Asset Alloc. -5.8%	Asset Alloc. 6.2%	Large Cap 14.5%
7	Large Cap 10.9%	Small Cap 4.6%	High Yield 13.7%	Cash 4.8%	Comdty. -35.6%	Asset Alloc. 25.0%	Asset Alloc. 13.3%	Small Cap -4.2%	Asset Alloc. 12.2%	Cash 0.0%	Cash 0.0%	High Yield -2.7%	Asset Alloc. 8.3%	REITs 8.7%	Small Cap -11.0%	DM Equity 5.2%	High Yield 11.0%
8	Comdty. 9.1%	High Yield 3.6%	Cash 4.8%	High Yield 3.2%	REITs -37.7%	Comdty. 18.9%	DM Equity 8.2%	DM Equity -11.7%	Fixed Income 4.2%	Fixed Income -2.0%	EM Equity -1.8%	Small Cap -4.4%	Fixed Income 2.6%	Fixed Income 3.5%	Comdty. -11.2%	Fixed Income 3.9%	Asset Alloc. 10.3%
9	Fixed Income 4.3%	Cash 3.0%	Fixed Income 4.3%	Small Cap -1.6%	DM Equity -43.1%	Fixed Income 5.9%	Fixed Income 6.5%	Comdty. -13.3%	Cash 0.1%	EM Equity -2.3%	DM Equity -4.5%	EM Equity -14.6%	DM Equity 1.5%	Comdty. 1.7%	DM Equity -13.4%	Cash 1.3%	Fixed Income 3.3%
10	Cash 1.2%	Fixed Income 2.4%	Comdty. 2.1%	REITs -15.7%	EM Equity -53.2%	Cash 0.1%	Cash 0.1%	EM Equity -18.2%	Comdty. -1.1%	Comdty. -9.5%	Comdty. -17.0%	Comdty. -24.7%	Cash 0.3%	Cash 0.8%	EM Equity -14.2%	Comdty. -2.5%	Cash 0.8%

Investing principles

Source: J.P. Morgan Asset Management

As you can see from this chart, it's nearly impossible to accurately predict which asset class will be the best performer from one year to the next. Unfortunately, too many people fail to heed this advice, opting instead to stick with the results of their representative bias, failing to diversify in favor of return chasing.

To overcome the adverse result of representativeness bias, make sure you identify appropriate long-term investments by using a diversified asset allocation strategy that will increase the likelihood of better long-term portfolio returns that meets your financial goals. Then stick with it.

Anchoring and Adjustment Bias

The anchoring and adjustment bias occurs when an individual makes new decisions based on old or anchored information. For example, we see many people clinging to the purchase price or arbitrary price levels or price indexes when facing questions like, "Should I buy or sell this security?" or "Is the market overvalued or undervalued right now?"

This was evident during the housing crisis. A house value that inflated to $1 million just before the crisis may only have been worth $750,000 in normal market conditions. Owners still anchored their property value at $1 million. This is an example of how people tend to cling to the purchase price or arbitrary price level of an asset. The property was never worth $1 million, but in the owner's mind, it's anchored there because at one point they could sell it for that much. When the market crashed, people everywhere had trouble adjusting their mind to that reality.

It's important to consciously ask questions that may reveal an anchoring and adjustment bias. Always ask: Am I holding onto this stock based on rational analysis, or am I trying to attain a price that I am anchored to, such as the purchase price or a high water mark?

Remember that past prices, market levels, and reputation provide little information about an investment's future potential and thus should not influence buy-and-sell decisions to any great extent. Therefore, it is advisable to consider a typical research process: establish some sort of baseline expectation of an economic forecast or stock price, and then to adjust according to changes in those expectations. Always look at current information to reevaluate your initial estimate from time to time rather than simply anchoring future analysis around an initial study.

Always ask: Am I holding onto this stock based on rational analysis, or am I trying to attain a price that I am anchored to, such as the purchase price or a high water mark?

Mental Accounting Bias

Mental accounting bias is an information-processing bias in which people treat one sum of money differently from another equal-sized sum based on the mental account to which the money is assigned. They make the decision about what to do with the money differently depending on its source, for example, whether the money is from salary, a bonus, an inheritance, gambling winnings, or business profit. The accounts can also be mentally categorized based on the planned use of the money—for example, leisure or necessities.

For example, some people will put 10 percent of their salary away for retirement, but not 10 percent of a bonus. They think that since they're already saving from the salary, the bonus can be used for something else. When it comes to investments, people with this bias irrationally distinguish between returns derived from income and those derived from capital appreciation.

The total return of each investment has these two components: income and growth. Growth refers to the price going up. Income refers to the yield or rate of return that can be used as income to pay for expenses without touching the principal. Many people are so compelled to preserve capital (principal) that they focus on the idea of spending the income that the principal generates and can end up with investments that generate income but are not that good for growth. Junk bonds fall into this category. A junk bond is a low rating bond; it pays a much higher interest rate, potentially at least 6 percent, but there's not a lot of growth potential in the under-lying investment. An investor who wants high yield could end up with a lot of junk bonds that don't have long-term growth prospects rather than seeking out opportunities to reduce risk by combining assets with low correlations. Asset correlation is a measure of how and when investments move in relation to one another. A high cor-relation occurs when assets tend to move in the same direction at the same time, while a negative correlation occurs when one asset tends to move up when the other goes down.

An effective way to detect and overcome mental account-ing behavior is to recognize when you are not taking correlations between investments into account in your overall portfolio. To do this, combine all of your assets onto one spreadsheet to see the true asset allocation of various mental account holdings. Then, to avoid the trap of treating investment income and capital appreciation dif-ferently, think in terms of total return, and allocate enough assets to lower income investments such as stocks to allow the principal to continue to outpace inflation.

Loss-Aversion Bias

Loss-aversion bias is a bias in which people tend to strongly prefer avoiding losses as opposed to achieving gains. We have seen some new clients hold onto losers even if those stocks have little or no chance of recovering.

> *Some studies have suggested that the experience of losses is twice as powerful, psychologically, as gains.*

Some studies have suggested that the experience of losses is twice as powerful, psychologically, as gains.[14] The consequence of loss-aversion bias is that you can hold investments in a loss position longer than justified by fundamental analysis. Alternatively, you could sell investments in a gain position earlier than justified for fear that their profit will erode. It's also common that loss-averse investors will hold riskier portfolios than are acceptable to their risk/return objectives. The way to overcome loss-aversion bias is through education and seeking the counsel of a trusted advisor.

Final Thoughts

All humans have biases. We know they are a natural part of how our brain works. We also know that returns on long-term investments are impacted by the short-term beliefs, emotions, and impulses. Therefore, to ensure that your biases are not compromising your investment goals and ability to manage your wealth, you need to not only understand how capital markets work but also challenge any biases affecting your decisions.

14 D. Kahneman and A. Tversky, "Advances in prospect theory: Cumulative representation of uncertainty," *Journal of Risk and Uncertainty* 5, no. 4 (1992): 297–323.

Be mindful of the decisions that you're making. Strive to identify your biases by challenging them with the questions in this chapter. Look back on your decisions and their results and see how you can learn from those going forward. Ask yourself:

1. Which biases do I think I tend to have?
2. What are the challenges I have experienced recently to overcome the biases?
3. What was my worst investment decision, and what lessons have I learned from it?

Biases will always exist. Investing success is ultimately achieved by those who can conquer the daily psychological challenges and maintain a long-term perspective. This means understanding and challenging biases is an ongoing process as you build your wealth and your portfolio throughout your life so that you can finally reach your financial independence day. We will look at this in the next chapter.

CHAPTER 5

Financial Independence Day

If money and time were not an issue, what kind of activities would you be doing over the next twelve months?

The day when work becomes optional—when you can choose to stop working and start doing those activities that you enjoy while maintaining your current standard of living—is the day you've reached your financial independence day. This day is the end result of a process of determining your retirement income goals and the actions and decisions necessary to achieve those goals.

Retirement planning is, in essence, preparation for life after paid work ends, not just financially but in terms of lifestyle choices, such as how to spend time in retirement, where to live, when to completely quit working. When planning for retirement, a holistic approach is the right way to go.

Therefore, in the first part of this chapter, I will talk about preparing for retirement at different stages of your life by saving money and investing wisely so that you can realistically plan your way to financial independence. In the second part of this chapter, I'll offer planning tips and issues to think about in order to enjoy your retirement years.

A Plan for Every Stage of Life

People often deny themselves their dreams because they don't understand the resources needed. This is why it's important that I get their list of dreams during a discovery meeting in order to explore options and tell them what's realistic. If a goal is unrealistic based on current net worth, income, and expenses, I can make suggestions for changes to get them to a better place. I can run some scenarios to show if they are spending too much now to retire in their target year, and I can offer recommendations.

Financial independence isn't necessarily just about retirement. In an earlier chapter, Violet wanted the financial independence to pursue her new career goals. Another person may want to keep their job until they're sixty-five in order to know that they have a good retirement plan in place. It's important at any stage of life to think about your dream lifestyle and share those goals with a financial advisor/planner. From there, you can think about the timeline to your financial independence day and devise a realistic plan that also reflects your values, no matter what stage of your life you're currently in.

Planning for Financial Independence in Early Adulthood (Ages Twenty-One to Thirty-Five)

When you're in early adulthood, ages twenty-one to thirty-five, you have time on your side to put plans in place that will help you later. This makes your guidelines to financial independence a little different than those designed for older adults.

Mr. and Mrs. Navy came to my office ten years ago shortly after he started a new job as an ophthalmologist in his early thirties. He had a high income, but his medical school student loan balances were so large that their net worth was negative. Mrs. Navy was busy taking care of two young children at home. I helped them define short-term and long-term goals and designed a budget that would allow them to pay off student loan balances while saving for retirement in his 401(k) plan. Two years later, I helped him make the important decision to borrow money to buy into a profitable medical business when he was presented the opportunity to become a partner. Over the years, he earned a higher income than he would have from his salary alone because the business profit distributions were higher than projected. He decided to work extra hours by taking calls after regular office hours to earn even more income in order to pay off student and business loans sooner than projected. In addition to maximizing contributions to his 401(k) plan, I also set up an SEP IRA for him and maximized pretax contributions based on his on-call self-employment income.

The couple are now in their forties and have no debt except for their mortgage. They are on track to achieve their retirement and college funding goals. The initial planning and ongoing monitoring helped them focus on what they could control, such as performing well at work and saving regularly. It had been hard for them to talk about money and spending before working with me, but I was able to keep them motivated along the way.

TIPS IN EARLY ADULTHOOD (AGES TWENTY-ONE TO THIRTY-FIVE)

- Start saving and invest early, even with a small amount of money. Compound interest will work extremely well for you over time. Once you are earning income, start saving for an emergency fund in a savings account that can pay for at least three months of living expenses.

- Open a 401(k) plan and/or a Roth IRA. In the 401(k) plan, make sure you contribute enough to get all the matching contributions from your employer. If your employer matches $0.50 to $1.00 of contribution up to 6 percent of your pay, you must contribute at least 6 percent to get the full matching.

Start saving and invest early, even with a small amount of money. Compound interest will work extremely well for you over time.

- Hedge against a potential future tax rate hike by allocating some money to three types of accounts: tax-free accounts (HSA, Roth IRA, and Roth 401(k) accounts); tax-deferred accounts (pretax 401(k) and traditional IRA accounts); and taxable accounts (individual accounts, trust accounts, and joint accounts).

- If your income is low enough, contribute directly to a Roth IRA with after-tax dollars. Distributions from a Roth IRA after age 59.5 will be income-tax-free, which makes a Roth

IRA a good choice when you are at the beginning of your career and have a lower income level but expect to be in a higher tax bracket during retirement.

- Form healthy money habits by creating a monthly spending plan. Consider using www.mint.com to link up checking, credit cards, and your mortgage account to track actual expenses against your spending plan. List your savings goals, and make saving in them systematic as you do with your monthly rent or mortgage.

- Create and maintain good credit scores. Use www.annual-creditreport.com or www.creditkarma.com to check and monitor your scores annually for free.

Planning for Financial Independence in Early Midlife (Ages Thirty-Six to Fifty)

Most people who come to a financial planner tend to think they can't become financially independent, at least not when they want. They don't know what to do now to make it possible later, as was the case of Mr. and Mrs. Black.

In their early forties, the Blacks came to me, hoping to fully fund the private school and college education of two children and also explore the possibility of early retirement. Of their entire portfolio, 80 percent was invested in the stock of one company; let's call it ABC. Mrs. Black's father had given the stock to her, and it had performed well over the years. She had been the director of market research for a *Fortune* 500 company for twenty years and had accumulated employer's stock inside her 401(k) plan because the company matched employees' contributions each year with stock in the company. She was not confident about making financial decisions and was fearful of making the wrong move, which meant she never sold any shares. She ended up with 13 percent of her portfolio in her company's stock, which meant, overall, she had 93 percent of her portfolio invested in only two companies.

The Blacks were also charitable people but hadn't donated in a tax-efficient way.

It was important to devise a plan to support their retirement at fifty-five and ensure they had enough money to last them until ninety-five. It was also important to find a way to turn her $10,000-a-year charitable donations into a tax benefit. She had been paying over 45 percent total income tax and payroll taxes on her salary and was donating cash to United Way through payroll deductions.

Had Mrs. Black sold any of her ABC stock in her brokerage account, she would have owed taxes on the long-term capital gains (about 33 percent combining federal and Minnesota state taxes), but if she moved this appreciated ABC stock to her donor-advised fund, there would be no tax reporting obligation when she sold the stock within this account. A donor-advised fund allows donors to make a charitable contribution of assets or cash and take an income tax deduction immediately. They can then recommend grants to their favorite charities whenever they want. In this case, Mrs. White would get a $200,000 charitable deduction on her tax returns because she gave up stock that was worth $200,000 on the date of gift. The cost basis of this stock donation was only about $20,000. She also saved the capital gains taxes (about $59,400) on the $180,000 long-term capital gains because the gains realized by selling the stock inside the donor-advised fund are not taxable to her. If she gave 5 percent of the balance (i.e., about $10,000 per year) to charities, her account could continue to grow or sustain itself to benefit charities in the long term.

Down the road, she could add more stocks to her donor-advised fund when she wanted to reduce her taxable income and increase her annual grants to charities. If she continued donating cash to charities through payroll deductions or writing checks, she could deduct the cash as charitable deductions, but not save on the capital gains taxes on the sale of this stock and would lose out on the potential growth from this tax savings. When we ran these scenarios in the dashboard, this tax efficiency contributed greatly to her being able to achieve her retirement goals over time while continuing to meet her current charitable giving goal.

A 529 plan was the answer to her college funding goals. A 529 plan, or "qualified tuition plan," is a tax-advantaged savings plan designed to encourage saving for future education costs. They are sponsored by states, state agencies, or educational institutions and are authorized by Section 529 of the Internal Revenue Code.[15] Contributions to the 529 plans are made with after-tax dollars, but the balance can grow tax-free to pay for qualified expenses including college tuition, books and supplies, and room and board. If you invest the money in your individual brokerage account, you would pay taxes every year on realized gains, interest, and dividends, thus growing at a lower rate than investing in a tax-free 529 plan. Recent tax law changes allow tax-free withdrawals to pay for private school (K to 12) qualified expenses of up to $10,000 per person per year.

We also set up two traditional IRAs and advised the Blacks to maximize their nondeductible contributions to their IRAs. We later converted the balance of the IRAs to Roth IRAs so that they had more money in the tax-free Roth IRA accounts. We will look at tax strategies in more detail in chapter 8.

15 US Securities and Exchange Commission, "An introduction to 529 plans" (May 29, 2018). Available at https://www.sec.gov/reportspubs/investor-publications/investorpubsintro529htm.html.

She had 100 percent of her portfolio in the stock market, and 93 percent of that was spread across just two stocks; therefore, by diversifying, we also reduced her portfolio risk to be much closer to her risk aversion score, which was lower than average.

Once all of this data was included in the tool, we ran the "what if" scenarios. For example, what will happen if you lose your job? We looked at what kind of pension she'd get, how that would affect her retirement goals, and what adjustments she would have to make to stay on track. This not only helped her keep her goals in sight, but it also helped her maintain her risk tolerance by making her better prepared for a job transition should that situation arise.

As the case of the Blacks shows, when planning your financial independence day, it's important to establish your primary goals and then implement some changes to get you closer to that place. This might mean knowing the best time to exercise nonqualified stock options (NSOs) provided to you by your employer and know the tax impact of exercising stock options before their expiration date. You don't pay taxes when you receive NSOs or when they vest, but you pay income taxes and payroll taxes when you exercise them by buying the shares at the grant price when the market price is greater than the grant price. Closely monitoring stock options two years before expiration date is critical because the in-the-money value of the stock options is more sensitive to stock price change as they approach the expiration date. It was important to have the data and tools in place to help her maximize the value of the stock options before they expired.

PLANNING TIPS IN EARLY MIDLIFE (AGES THIRTY-SIX TO FIFTY)

- Continue to fund your 401(k) plan. Consider maximizing contributions as your income increases. In 2019, the maximum contribution by an employee is $19,000. If you are age fifty and above, you can contribute an additional $6,000 (in catch-up contributions) per year.

- Consider choosing an HDHP instead of a traditional health insurance plan to save on monthly premiums. Maximize contributions to a health savings account (HSA) because they are tax deductible. The balance in the HSA can be invested and grow tax-free to pay for your qualified medical expenses now or during retirement.

- If you have limited income and didn't start saving for retirement until your midthirties, consider increasing retirement savings before saving for college because many institutions will lend money to your children for higher education, but no one will lend you money to retire. Otherwise, consider funding a college savings account (a 529 plan).

- Make sure you have proper life insurance and disability insurance so that your loved ones don't have to withdraw early from retirement accounts should something happen to you.

- If your income is too high to contribute directly to a Roth IRA, consider funding a traditional IRA (maximum of $6,000 in 2019; $7,000 for age fifty and over). IRA contributions may not be tax deductible due to income limitations if you participate in a 401(k) plan, but traditional IRA contributions are worth making because the earnings are tax deferred and you can convert the balance later to a Roth IRA.

Planning for Financial Independence in Late Midlife (Ages Fifty-One to Sixty-Five)

Mr. White discovered that for those approaching retirement age, it's important to include Social Security planning in the overall retirement plan.

Mr. White came to me when he was ready to retire from a corporate job. His wife, who was fourteen years his junior, had a part-time job. He was extremely organized and had made all his own investment decisions throughout his life, but he wanted to make sure there was an advisor and a plan for his wife, who hadn't the confidence to make financial decisions, in the event of his death.

We took inputs from both of them to create and update a plan. He is healthy, but we had to factor in the possibility of him dying first. Our challenge, therefore, was to devise a plan to help them maximize their Social Security benefits.

Many people start taking Social Security at sixty-two, but this offers a reduced monthly benefit. However, it's possible to delay collecting this retirement money until the full retirement age (FRA) of age sixty-five or later based on year of birth. For every year you delay past your FRA up to age seventy, you get an 8 percent increase in your benefit every year. If your FRA is sixty-six, delaying to age seventy will increase your monthly benefit by 32 percent. If you claim Social Security at age sixty-two, rather than waiting until FRA, you can expect up to a 30 percent reduction in monthly benefits.

I recommended that Mr. White delay collecting Social Security and showed him how much more he would benefit by waiting until age seventy. His family tended to live long lives, so if, like them, he were also to live twenty years past retirement, he would still be able to collect a lot of money. Additionally in his case, with a wife fourteen years younger, she would be able to collect higher survivors benefits during her lifetime.

As the Whites discovered, factoring Social Security planning into their overall retirement plan was important. An advantage of Social Security over the annuities you can buy in the market is that it has inflation adjustments over time. This means you can afford a little bit more risk in your investment portfolio because you have some guaranteed income for life that could help you pay for basic expenses, shelter, and food. We advised the Whites to use the money in their investment accounts to supplement his pension income by delaying collecting his Social Security benefit until age seventy.

PLANNING TIPS IN LATE MIDLIFE (AGES FIFTY-ONE TO SIXTY-FIVE)

- As you are approaching retirement, your investment risk tolerance should be lower in order to avoid losing too much right before you retire or in the early years of retirement when you don't have the luxury of time to wait for a market upswing.[16]

- These may be your high-income years, so maximize the catch-up contributions to your 401(k) plan and your IRA.

- Consider buying long-term-care insurance to reduce your long-term-care expenses when you are still healthy and you are on track with your retirement savings.[17]

- You cannot enroll in Medicare until age sixty-five, so if you retire before sixty-five, your financial plan needs to include some estimations of additional health insurance costs for the

16 See chapter 6 on investment planning for more information.

17 See chapter 9 on long-term-care insurance for more information.

years that you have retired without an insurance plan provided by an employer. Review your health insurance choices, including your employer's plan, and consider choosing a high deductible health plan combined with an HSA.

- Include Social Security planning in your overall retirement plan. If you have other resources, it's best not to take Social Security benefits before your full retirement age because the benefits will be greatly reduced. You can maximize the survivors benefit that is available by having the highest earner of the two wait until age seventy to begin benefits. It creates a larger monthly benefit amount that becomes the survivors benefit when the first spouse passes.

Planning for Eight Thousand Days

MIT produced a paper that claimed that the average retirement span is eight thousand days,[18] which means it's important to consider the quality of your retirement life for that length of time. In this section, I'll offer planning tips in order to enjoy your retirement years.

Every retirement plan should have a realistic allowance for lifestyle expenses. People often do a lot more travel in the first year of retirement. Health insurance usually becomes a factor in a retirement plan. Employers generally pay most of the cost of health insurance, but in the event of loss of job or retirement, the individual will have to cover that cost themselves. A person must be sixty-five to enroll in Medicare. Therefore, we must consider health insurance choices as an expense for retirement years.

18 AgeLabs divided the eight thousand days into four stages; eight thousand days can be broken into four separate phases, each with its own set of challenges. For more information, see: http://agelab.mit.edu/system/files/2018-12/8000_days_workbook_0.pdf.

Another important question is this: Where do you want to live during retirement? Where the client sees themselves living is an important part of the plan, including the possible decision to downsize and free up more assets from the sale of their home and the resulting reduction in expenses, such as property taxes and insurance. However, there are other factors to consider in terms of location. For example, people often have lofty ideas about the location to which they'll retire. Some people want to retire to the mountains and to nature, which is a lovely idea at fifty-five, but at seventy-five or eighty, it may prevent you from having access to the services you need. Is your area of choice one where you can have easy access to the simple things in life as you age? Is your home close to or far from your social network? There are more factors at play than simply a calm and scenic view.

When it comes to retirement planning, we're inclined to focus on accumulating assets and making sure we spend our money wisely. But while our biggest fear may be outliving our wealth, there's an even greater risk of losing our independence due to ailing health, being unable to access the big and small things that make us happy, and facing a decline in the number of friends in our social network. We'll revisit this subject again in chapter 9 ("Long-Term Care").

Thinking about a Realistic Retirement Plan

Three questions can predict how realistic your retirement plan is and how manageable it looks: Who will change my light bulbs? How will I get ice cream cones? Whom will I have lunch with?

WHO WILL CHANGE MY LIGHT BULBS?

Many people may someday lose their independence due to health conditions. At some point, it will become dangerous to climb a ladder to change a light bulb, which means many people will need to have a plan in place to maintain their home that includes maintenance costs and has identified trusted service providers. This is as critical to aging independently as having health insurance and retirement savings. If the plan shows the home will be too hard to maintain, then it's important to think of an alternative way of living.

HOW WILL I GET ICE CREAM CONES?

How you will get ice cream cones (or how accessible the things you want will be) is the second question to ask before heading into retirement. How will you manage simple things, like getting groceries or finding the transportation to do something you like if you can no longer drive? Without this access, you may not enjoy your retirement.

WHOM WILL I HAVE LUNCH WITH?

In retirement, your social network may shrink because people have fewer activities as they age. Today, in particular, if a person doesn't actively create a social network, they could find themselves lonely in retirement. Loneliness can kill, which means it's important not only to have friends online, but friends you see on a regular basis. Having people to have lunch with can reinforce a healthy and active lifestyle.

During a discovery meeting and in later meetings to update your financial independence plan, it's important to look at these issues as part of your goals. Your numbers might look great in the dashboard today and projected till the age of ninety-five, but it's also important to think about where you plan to buy a second home for retirement and take these three questions into account.

I also advise clients that it's not enough to spend a few days or weeks in an ideal spot; they should live there for several months in a rental before deciding to buy in order to have a grasp of accessibility, transportation, activities they enjoy, and the social network in the area. Accessibility to children and grandchildren may also be a factor.

Women's Unique Challenges

In the past two decades, as I have helped clients plan for their financial independence day, I've noticed that women face unique challenges.

First, women today work about twelve years less than men, mainly due to having caregiving responsibilities for children, relatives, spouses, and parents. Second, according to the US Census Bureau, women had median weekly earnings that were 82 percent of those of their male counterparts.[19] Since Social Security and many employer retirement benefits are tied to earnings, women end up with lower levels of guaranteed retirement income. As a result, women's median income in retirement is only 58 percent of men's. Third, women live longer than men, so their money must last longer. Fourth, women are more comfortable talking about money with female financial planners and are more inclined to seek help from women, but only 23 percent of CFP® practitioners are women. Only about 20 percent of all financial advisors/planners in the US have the CFP® designation. In other words, there simply aren't enough CFP® practitioners to serve women.

There are, however, some practical tips that women can implement on their own.

---

19 US Bureau of Labor Statistics, Report 1069, "Highlights of women's earnings in 2016" (August 2017). Available at https://www.bls.gov/opub/reports/womens-earnings/2016/pdf/home.pdf.

Six Tips Specifically for Women

If you are a woman, the first tip to reaching your financial independence day is to start retirement saving early in your career because you have fewer years in the workforce. This is essential for long-term financial health.

Second, if you are a married women, it's important to actively participate in financial planning and not leave it totally to your spouse. Engage in the conversations about how you feel about your money and your short-term and long-term goals when you and your spouse work with a planner. Women have different concerns compared to men about their retirement years, and if they are not participating in the discussion and planning, their concerns will not be addressed. Generally speaking, women are more concerned about planning for potential long-term-care expenses. In addition, they are more concerned about outliving their money. They tend to be more open to buying long-term-care insurance in order to share the risk with an insurance company or to buying an annuity to increase their guaranteed lifetime income.

If you are a woman, the first tip to reaching your financial independence day is to start retirement saving early in your career because you have fewer years in the workforce. This is essential for long-term financial health.

Third, in my experience, we live in a culture in which it's believed that men are better with investments, including picking stocks. Women therefore all too often leave financial decisions to their spouses, no matter how smart or successful they are in their careers.

I've noticed that the financial landscape then becomes frightening to women when they become widows. For this reason, it's important to participate in all financial decisions as early as possible.

Fourth, women should not overlook their physical health. Health is a valuable asset in your financial strategy. Women who invest in maintaining healthy lifestyles can enjoy better health with lower medical expenses for decades. In other words, health and wealth go together, and investing in the former is as important as investing in the latter.

Underestimating life expectancy is another issue about which women need to be mindful. Although the average life expectancy in the United States is currently eighty-one for women and seventy-six for men, statistics show that a person has a fifty-fifty chance of living past age ninety if they have already reached the age of sixty-five.[20] As such, the Echo Dashboard projects a financial picture until the age of ninety-five to show how a desired standard of living can be maintained for the long term.

The fifth tip for women is having a balanced plan. As with Mr. and Mrs. Black, who wanted a college fund and charitable giving in retirement, a growth investment strategy needs to be put in place to keep up with inflation so that guaranteed income from pension, Social Security, and annuities can help them pay for basic expenses after retirement. Putting in place adequate insurance protection in the event of significant losses, such as life insurance, disability insurance, and long-term-care insurance, is key.

Sixth, it's important to consult an expert. As we saw in the last chapter, while wealth management doesn't have to be complicated when working with a trusted expert and the team, financial products

20 Steve Vernon, "How much longer might you live? Think again," CBS News, October 16, 2014. Available at https://www.cbsnews.com/news/two-common-mistakes-we-make-thinking-about-how-long-we-might-live/.

are getting more complicated. Therefore, instead of doing nothing, it's better to talk to a few financial advisors to find a partnership that is a good fit for you.

Final Thoughts

There is no way to avoid meticulous planning when you are trying to reach your financial independence day. No matter where you are or what your net worth is, having a plan at whatever stage of life you are, even if it's not perfect, is critical to getting you on the right path.

It's also important to recognize the roadblocks on your path. Ask yourself:

1. What are the biggest challenges you face?

2. Have you done any planning to address these? For example, if college funding is a goal, have you consulted anyone about making this provision in your plan?

3. If retirement planning confuses you, have you identified someone you can trust to offer advice? If you are still in the job market, do you have an alternative means of generating income from other assets in case of emergency?

Meticulous planning can start anytime in life, but starting now will make a big difference down the road. Burying your head in the sand is the last thing you should do. It's never too early to start recognizing gaps and filling them in your plan. For example, if you don't have a budget, it's time to start working on one. If you don't have a projection tool or a financial advisor, find a tool online that will help you calculate how much you need to have by a certain age in order to retire. If you don't know how to do it, finding a trusted advisor should be your first order of business.

Other questions to ask yourself are as follows:

1. Have you written down your goals?

2. If you have nonqualified stock options, are you monitoring them in a timely manner, and do you have a strategy in place?

3. As you approach retirement, will you stay in your home or downsize? Will you travel extensively the first ten years of retirement?

These answers will also help you determine how much you need to make work optional.

Finally, it's important to think about how you're going to spend your time. To go from being a busy working person to being retired requires a lot more than preretirement planning. Net worth, income, and expenses will need to be continually monitored.

As you can see, there are many moving pieces in getting to your financial independence day. If it seems too complicated, remember that it doesn't have to be. Turn to a team of trusted advisors to help you on your way. I'll talk about what you should look for in a team in chapter 7, but first let's look at investment planning and risk tolerance.

CHAPTER 6

Five Steps to a Solid Investment Plan

Too often I see people buying a random collection of funds and stocks without any particular framework or investment strategy. They have goals, but there's often a mismatch among those objectives, their financial resources, and their risk tolerance. In other words, they don't have a viable investment plan.

In order to reach your required rate of return to achieve retirement or other financial goals, you must work on financial planning, and to do this well, you must understand the five basic steps required, regardless of whether you are working alone or with a financial advisor.

Step 1. Goal Setting and Preparing an Investment Plan

The first step toward creating a solid financial plan involves setting goals. At Echo Wealth Management, we like to learn about clients' dreams and goals in addition to gathering their financial data in order to implement a customized financial plan to realize them. We also assess clients' risk tolerance, time frame until they need to start withdrawing, and how much they need from their portfolio. A good financial advisor will never skip the planning phase, so make sure your financial advisor covers all these bases.

Once we have dreams and data in place, it's time to use a tool like the Echo Dashboard to run different scenarios to explore outcomes based on changes in risk tolerance, revised expenses, or changes in return on investment (ROI) expectations. Exploring scenarios and determining the outcome of different strategies and decisions is the best way to begin to build a solid and achievable financial plan.

Step 2. How to Think about Risk

Every investment has risks. The usual pattern is that when the stock market goes up, the bond market goes down (usually due to the Federal Reserve Bank increasing interest rates), but market cycles can be very strange indeed. In 2018, both the stock and bond markets lost money. This is precisely why everyone needs a solid education in investment planning, whether working alone or with an advisor, in order to determine risk tolerance and, on that basis, the right asset allocation to maximize after-tax risk-adjusted return.

Risk tolerance is a critical ingredient in any investment plan, but contrary to widely held beliefs, risk doesn't mean risking the loss of all your money. It refers to volatility or a temporary value change in your portfolio. Therefore, the question to ask when preparing your investment plan is not can you tolerate the loss of your investment, but rather how much of a swing in value can you tolerate?

Fortunately, there are tools on the market to help you identify your tolerance level by assigning you a number that can then be used by your advisor to design the right asset allocation for you.

RISK NUMBER

Picking investments that are riskier than you can tolerate can lead to some ugly outcomes. Often in market downturns, people see a 50 percent drop in their portfolio, and they panic and start to sell, which, as mentioned in chapter 4 on behavioral biases, is precisely the wrong time to sell. On the flip side, choosing investments that are not risky enough—that is, that do not have the high potential for growth—can be a roadblock to reaching your financial goals.

Discovering your risk tolerance doesn't have to be a trial and error process. Tools such as Riskalyze are available to help you. Riskalyze offers you a detailed questionnaire from which it calculates a risk number that reflects your *willingness* to take risk. Generalizing a client's risk tolerance doesn't work. Risk is personal, and it needs to be viewed through a client's own unique lens to gauge risk and return trade-offs. Therefore, we look at how much risk clients can handle over the short term to hit their long-term objectives.

The Case of Mr. Brown

A new client, fifty-six-year-old Mr. Brown, did the Riskalyze detailed questionnaire before deciding to retire. Based on a portfolio of $6.2 million and a six-month comfort zone (range of return with 95 percent probability: a loss of 10.16 percent and gain of 16.04 percent), the tool calculated his risk number to be 52. The risk number is calculated based on downside risk. On a scale from 1 to 99, the greater the potential loss, the greater the risk number. Riskalyze presents multiple questions about investors' preferred rate of return over a period of six months similar to this one: Do you want to choose certain return of 10 percent or 50 percent chance of losing 38.46 percent and 50 percent chance of gaining 150 percent? If you choose the latter, you may be asked another question, such as: Do you want to choose certain loss of 14.23 percent or 50 percent chance of losing 38.46 percent and 50 percent chance of gaining 150 percent? A maximum of fifteen questions is asked in different ways to see how much loss (percentage and dollar amount based on your portfolio size) you are willing to tolerate. Mr. Brown said $1 million would be a devastating loss to him, which meant he could not adopt an investment strategy that had this potential. His acceptable six-month risk is negative $629,920 (i.e., a loss of 10.16 percent).

The average risk profile is 52. Think of risk numbers like a bell curve: most people are in the 45–60 range, but not many have a high risk tolerance score of 85 or low risk tolerance score of 20. This means there is a good chance that you, like Mr. Brown, are in the curve range of 45–60. Had Mr. Brown's number been a very low risk number of 35, it would have been important to give him more information on short-term volatility and also the long-term returns for stocks and bonds in order for him to get comfortable taking a little bit more risk. We'll discuss volatility in the next section.

Many investors fear volatility in the market because they worry a market downturn would erase their hard-earned savings, but there is no need to fear volatility.

To work with the risk number 52 for Mr. Brown, we devised an investment portfolio that had a comparable risk level. We created a blended benchmark of 40 percent in the S&P 500 index, 40 percent in the US aggregated bond index, and 20 percent in the international

MSEI ACWI index (large and midcap representation across twenty-three developed markets and twenty-four emerging markets). The risk of spreading a portfolio across these three indices was equivalent to a risk number of 51, which meant the performance of this benchmark was roughly the same as his risk profile. This portfolio had a potential annual return of 6.2 percent before expenses, which exceeded his target nominal rate of return of 5 percent (net of expenses) for his financial plan prepared in his Echo Dashboard.

With this investment plan in place, he looked at different scenarios in the dashboard. He then realized that he could meet his retirement goals without cutting back on expenses. Many people make the mistake of thinking they need to assume more risk to reach their goals, but the case of Mr. Brown, it wasn't necessary to assume more risk than he could tolerate. There are always other options to consider.

VOLATILITY

Many investors fear volatility in the market because they worry a market downturn would erase their hard-earned savings, but there is no need to fear volatility. Yes, it presents risk in the short term, but it also creates opportunities for investors with a long-term horizon to get into the market at attractive price levels. For example, a stock options strategy may be a good nontraditional investment approach that can help you both reduce risk and increase your profits in a volatile market.

Options allow an investor to buy (call) or sell (put) a security at a predetermined price (strike price) on or before a specific date (expiration date).[21] Let's say, for example, that you inherited twenty thousand shares of ABC stock from your father, who had worked for ABC. You are aware that owning so much of one stock may be risky,

---

21 Michael Kramer, "Stock Option Definitions," *Investopedia* (April 20, 2019). Available at https://www.investopedia.com/terms/s/stockoption.asp.

but the current market price is at a historically low $25 per share, and you believe it is undervalued now based on your analysis, making selling unappealing. You would consider selling at $27 per share if you could get it. In this scenario, you or your advisor could find a buyer in the options market who is willing to pay you $20,000 today for the right to buy this stock (twenty thousand shares) from you at $27 anytime within the next six months. The buyer of the call option is under no obligation to buy the stock and can walk away, but if the stock price goes higher than $27, the buyer may decide to exercise his right to buy this stock for $27 before the expiration date.

As the seller of a call option, you have three possible outcomes:

1. The value of ABC stock rises over the next six months, and the buyer exercises his option to buy your stock for a total of $540,000 ($27 x 20,000 shares). You are better off by $40,000 ($540,000–$500,000) than if you had sold it on day 1 at $25 per share.

2. The price of ABC stock drops over the next six months. The buyer will likely walk away from the deal, and you still own the shares. While your stock is now worth less than it was on day 1, you get to keep the $20,000 cash premium you received for the option, which means you have reduced your loss with the $20,000.

3. The third possible outcome is that the value of ABC stock remains the same. The buyer of the option probably will not buy this stock for $27 per share and will walk away from the deal, but you have earned $20,000 cash in a flat market, and you still own these stocks.

This example is known as a covered call option strategy. In volatile markets, the premium tends to be higher, and so the option seller (you) can earn a nice income just by selling options on stocks already owned. There are many options strategies available to enhance your portfolio return or reduce losses. Therefore, don't fear volatility, and learn more about ways to embrace volatility to your advantage.

TIME FRAME AND WITHDRAWAL

Once you've taken the first step to identify your risk number, the next step is to identify your time frame to withdrawal in order to adjust your investment plan in a way that will allow you to achieve your long-term goals. For example, if you need an annual return of 5 percent to achieve your long term goals and have fifteen years to reach that goal, a lower-risk portfolio of 30 percent in stock markets and 70 percent in bonds may not be the optimal allocation for you. Moving more money into stocks, while traditionally riskier than bonds, has the potential to grow in value and pay dividends, and because you have fifteen years before you begin to withdraw, you have time for your portfolio to recover in the event of a market downturn before you need to make a withdrawal.

Long-term investors are in a position to allocate a larger portion of their portfolio in higher-risk investments, such as stocks, because a longer time horizon is associated with lower volatility. You can see the range of stocks, bonds, and blended total return 1950–2018 in the following chart.[22] Stock returns can vary greatly (e.g., if you only have a one-year time horizon, you could lose 39 percent). However, if you have a ten-year time horizon, the worst return is negative 1 percent. However, it's important to remember to measure performance within the context of your investment strategy. For example, it's not practical to expect returns on par with Dow Jones Industrial

22 J.P. Morgan, "Guide to the Markets" (March 31, 2019). Available at https://am.jpmorgan.com/blob-gim/1383407651970/83456/MI-GTM_2Q19_%20LINKED.pdf.

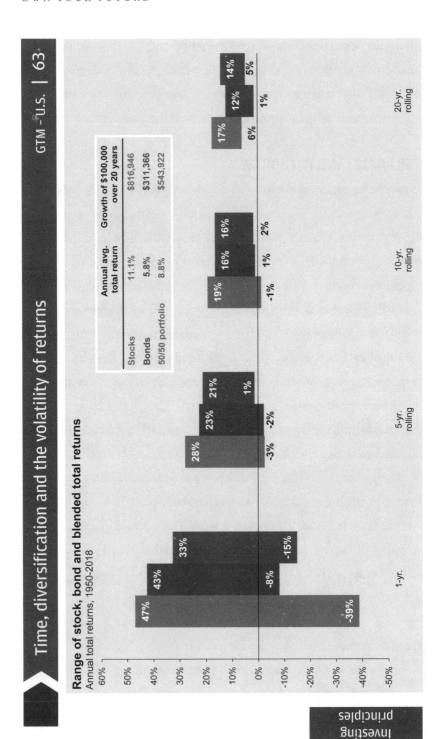

Source: J.P. Morgan Asset Management

Average or S&P 500 Index if your portfolio consists of various stocks, bonds, and alternatives that seek to provide risk-adjusted returns. This is another reason why it's important for your advisor point out any mismatch between your own risk number and the risk number associated with your portfolio.

On the other end of the spectrum to the risk averse client is the client who has a high risk tolerance but doesn't have the resources to afford taking high risks, either because of a too-small portfolio or too few years to retirement (the fewer years to retirement, the less time the market has to recover after a decline). The lack of time and assets coupled with an unwillingness to cut back on discretionary living expenses or an inability to further tighten a budget means there's not a lot of fat to cut if this client wants to retire in two years. This kind of client may want to make high-risk choices, but the time and resources aren't there to help him or her achieve potential high returns. We generally must educate this type of client and use budgeting tools to help them save more soon and help them choose the combination of delaying target retirement date, increasing retirement income by working part time, and reducing expenses because it would not be wise to count on unrealistic investment returns.

In short, there are three points to remember when devising your investment plan:

1. Different types of investments have different levels of risk.

2. The longer you keep your money invested, the better your chances of overcoming a declining market.

3. Your investment gains can grow exponentially over time as your earnings are compounded, for example, a 5 percent rate of return over twenty years can move you significantly closer to your financial independence goals.

Step 3. Portfolio Construction

Your ideal asset allocation is the mix of investments, from most aggressive to safest, that will earn the total return over time that you need. Once you have identified your target risk number and asset allocation, it's time to identify an appropriate combination of securities in various retirement and nonretirement accounts in your portfolio.

There are endless combinations when constructing a portfolio. The securities you can select include mutual funds, exchange traded funds (ETFs), individual stocks, and bonds. You must do research on a wide range of securities to select the ones you want to buy to build your portfolio. After you have decided what securities to buy, review them to decide how they should be held inside tax-deferred, tax-free, and taxable accounts.

In general, when constructing your own investment plan, it's important to determine how much to allocate to the three major categories: stocks (for growth), bonds (for income), and cash (for capital preservation). Bonds with different maturity dates are part of your fixed income allocation; they do not grow as much as stocks, but they pay 2 percent to 5 percent annualized income subject to credit quality, liquidity, and duration. Cash means checking, savings, and money market funds that provide you the liquidity you need with minimal return. Stocks are your main growth investment, but you should have a ten-year or longer time frame before you need to sell because a major market downturn, such as the 2007–08 financial crisis, could be five years away and may take four or five years to recover.

As part of your investment plan, your cash flow plan should include the projected amounts you need to withdraw from your portfolio per year after receiving Social Security, pension, or annuity income. As you live in retirement, you'll need to sell equity or fixed income securities to rebalance your portfolio and park more in cash (about one year's worth of expenses) for withdrawals.

At Echo Wealth Management, we have developed a framework to determine the best combination of securities in order to construct a customized portfolio that addresses equity needs, manages distribution requirements, and monitors allocation. It helps us create a plan that is low cost, tax efficient, and diversified in order to accommodate clients' goals, resources, time frame, and risk number. It includes low-cost, tax-efficient ETFs to build a portfolio because large company stocks in most markets are relatively efficient, as are the markets themselves. While results of short-term may be favorable, the majority of active equity funds underperform their benchmarks over a long-term investment horizon.[23] In other words, the odds you'll do better than an index fund (or an index ETF) are close to 1 in 20 when picking an actively managed domestic equity mutual fund.

I'm not aware of any way of identifying in advance the select active mutual funds that will be able to beat the market over the long term. In fact, S&P Global found that there's a stronger likelihood that a top performing fund will become one of the worst performers in a subsequent period than that it will stay a top performer.

Owning index funds and index ETFs representing various asset classes—including US large cap, midcap, and small cap—is more likely to generate results that match the markets. To add more diversification to your portfolio, it's best to actively manage some alternative investments, including hedged equity funds, managed futures funds,

---

23 Over the fifteen-year investment horizon, 92.33 percent of large-cap managers, 94.81 percent of midcap managers, and 95.73 percent of small-cap managers failed to outperform on a relative basis. See for more info https://us.spindices.com/documents/spiva/spiva-us-year-end-2017.pdf.

and funds that use index-based options to either enhance income (selling calls) or protect the downside (buying puts). Alternative investments including real estate involve complexity and generally higher expenses than index funds, and I recommend seeking professional advice when you want to add more diversification beyond stocks, bonds, and cash.

As you construct your portfolio, alone or with an advisor, it's important to remember to select an asset allocation that matches your risk profile and the rate of return you need to meet your goals.

DIVERSIFICATION

Some people have fears about managing money. Often, this is because they had a bad experience, made mistakes on their own, or worked with an advisor who didn't explain the risks and create a portfolio that sat comfortably with their risk tolerance level. The answer to this fear is creating a good blend of securities and being willing to take calculated risks across a diversified portfolio.

A 1986 landmark study by Gary P. Brinson, CFA, Randolph Hood, and Gilbert L. Beebower (known collectively as BHB)[24] investigated potential drivers of portfolio performance. What they found to be most important wasn't market timing or individual security selection but rather asset allocation across large, midsize, and small US companies and stocks and bonds in developed countries. They found that asset allocation drove 94 percent of portfolio performance. This means that it's not what you buy and sell but how you diversify across asset classes that has the biggest impact on your portfolio's long-term performance. In other words, the key to reducing risk is diversification.

24 Gary P. Brinson, CFA, Randolph Hood, and Gilbert L. Beebower, "Determinants of Portfolio Performance," *Financial Analysts Journal* 42, no. 4 (July/August 1986): 39–44. Available at https://www.cfapubs.org/doi/pdf/10.2469/faj.v42.n4.39.

For example, when our clients see their cash flow on the Echo Dashboard and see a detailed analysis of their current portfolio and their time frame and goals, they can see projections and the adjustments we can make to ensure they still meet

While many investors tend to buy domestic stock, it's a good idea to invest with a global perspective.

their retirement income needs in the long term. This tool shows them that their portfolios are adequately diversified so that should a bear market scenario arise, they are less likely to be forced to sell stocks, even if they incur a temporary loss of value. Showing detailed projected cash flow and withdrawals from various accounts for the next five years is key to building confidence in investment decisions.

INVESTING WITH A GLOBAL PERSPECTIVE

While many investors tend to buy domestic stock, it's a good idea to invest with a global perspective. This means understanding that emerging markets and developed markets, such as Europe, Japan, and Canada, also present opportunities.

When looking for global investment opportunities, it's important to look beyond projected GDP in these regions and pay attention to the valuation of the stocks you want to buy when they are relatively cheap compared to the long-term average. For example, as of December 31, 2018, the S&P 500 Index Forward P/E ratio (that is, price divided by earnings per share) was 14.4. The MSCI ACWI ex-US index (world stock excluding the US) had an 11.5 P/E ratio.[25] While US equity historically outperformed international equities, international stocks were about 20 percent cheaper than US stocks.

---

25 This compares to averages over the last twenty years; the average S&P 500 Index P/E was 15.8, while the MSCI ACWI Index was 14.2.

American investors tend to underweight emerging markets stocks, but it is advisable to have at least 10 percent of the stock portion of your portfolio in emerging markets stocks in order to potentially maximize return in the long term. China and India together constitute about 36 percent of the world's population. By 2030, emerging markets will account for 62 percent of total growth in global consumption. Anu Madgavka, a partner at McKinsey Global Institute, evaluated nearly seventy countries to identify the "overachievers" in emerging markets. Her team found that seven nations—China, South Korea, Singapore, Hong Kong, Malaysia, Indonesia, and Thailand—all had at least 3.5 percent real GDP growth per capita year-over-year for the past fifty years.[26]

If the dollar weakens or if US economic growth and earnings growth slow compared to overseas growth, the return on international equities is amplified. This means investing with a global perspective could be a solid strategy in your investment plan.

Step 4. Implementation

Implementation means executing your investment plan by buying and selling securities in various accounts. Since this involves a substantial amount of research, reading, and education, your advisor will often ask for discretionary trading authorization to make decisions on your behalf without getting approval for each individual trade. This makes finding a trusted financial advisor very important. I'll talk about this more in chapter 7 on your dream team.

26 Grace Donnelly, "This Is What the Fastest Growing Emerging Economies Have in Common," *Fortune* (October 17, 2018). http://fortune.com/2018/10/17/fastest-growing-emerging-economies/.

There are several areas that need to be considered before trading. These are asset location, cost basis review, concentrated stock position, and municipal bonds.

ASSET LOCATION

Where your advisor chooses to buy an investment and into what type of account is called asset location (as opposed to asset allocation, which refers to the rigorous implementation of an investment strategy that attempts to balance risk and reward by adjusting the percentage of each asset in an investment portfolio according to the investor's risk tolerance, goals, and investment time frame[27]).

Most clients have at least two types of accounts that have different tax treatments: tax-deferred, such as an IRA, or pretax 401(k), and taxable, such as an individual account, joint account, or revocable living trust account. Tax-deferred accounts allow you to defer any income and gains until you take distributions. Taxable accounts generate tax form 1099 every year to report interest, dividends, and realized capital gains or losses that you must report on your income tax returns. To maximize tax efficiency, proper asset location can generate an additional after-tax return when tax-inefficient assets are placed in the retirement accounts, and tax-efficient assets are placed in a taxable account.

For example, high-yield bonds pay interest that is taxable each year at an ordinary income tax rate if the bonds are held in a taxable account. A 5 percent return would become a 2.75 percent return after paying 45 percent in income taxes. However, holding high-yield bonds inside an IRA would not generate a tax bill until you take distributions from this IRA. Similarly, using options strategies would

27 For more information see: James Chen, "Asset Allocation," *Investopedia* (February 28, 2018). Available at https://www.investopedia.com/terms/a/assetallocation. asp#ixzz1QTuSzfhn.

generate more taxable income and these funds are more favorable to hold inside an IRA or a Roth IRA (tax-free account).

REVIEW COST BASIS, SHORT-TERM, OR LONG-TERM UNREALIZED GAINS

Part of implementing your investment plan means that you or your advisor should identify securities that should be sold immediately, such as those that are too high cost, have a poor track record, or do not fit your current investment plans. When reviewing your taxable accounts, any securities you decide to keep that have unrealized short-term gains that may turn into long-term gains soon should be held and monitored. If you sell a security with realized capital gains, this security needs to be held for at least a year to get the long-term capital gains tax treatment. The goal is to generate long-term gains instead of short-term gains in order to pay lower taxes because short-term gains are taxed at an ordinary federal income tax rate that could be as high as 37 percent, while the long-term federal capital gains rate is a maximum of 20 percent.

For example, if you bought ABC stock eleven months ago for $90,000, and it's now worth $100,000, you have an unrealized gain of $10,000. If you wait for one more month to sell, you'd pay a maximum of 20 percent ($2,000) in federal tax if the price doesn't change. If you sell it now, the $10,000 would be reported as short-term capital gains, and you'd pay up to 37 percent federal taxes ($3,700). Even if you are not at the top tax bracket, the difference between long-term gain tax rate and ordinary income tax rate is substantial.

CONCENTRATED STOCK POSITION

A concentrated stock position arises when you have a large portion (over 10 percent) of your stock portfolio in a single stock. This can happen often when people hold employer stock. This situation has a correlated risk because the person's human capital (i.e., ability to earn a living) is tied to the risk of the investment capital that you have saved for future retirement or other goals. Remember Enron? The employees not only lost their jobs, but they also lost the value of Enron stock inside their investment accounts.

Uncompensated risk is the level of additional risk for which no additional returns are generated on an investment. If you owned one stock with high concentration or too many stocks in a single market sector, you would have significant uncompensated risk. Modern portfolio theory divides risk into the categories of "compensated" and "uncompensated" risk. The risk of owning shares in a mature and well-managed company in a settled industry is less than the risk of owning shares in a start-up high-technology venture. The investor requires a higher expected return to induce the investor to bear the greater risk of disappointment associated with the start-up firm. This is compensated risk—the firm pays the investor for bearing the risk. By contrast, nobody pays the investor for owning too few stocks. Risk that can be eliminated by adding different stocks (or bonds) is uncompensated risk. The objective of diversification is to minimize this uncompensated risk.

Some clients are corporate officers for publicly traded companies, and they are required to hold some employer stock because of their positions, but the excess shares above the requirement should be sold at target prices outside the blackout periods to diversify and reduce risk. You can also reduce a concentrated stock position by setting up a donor-advised fund if you have charitable intent. You can donate some of the low-cost basis stock to your donor-advised fund and then benefit your favorite charities instead of writing checks to your charities. This will not only reduce your risk but will also reduce your tax bill.

MUNICIPAL BONDS

If you are a high-income professional living in a high-tax state like Minnesota and have a sizable taxable account (above $1 million), it's worth considering high-quality municipal bonds. If you buy your resident state's municipal bonds, the interest income from these bonds are income-tax-free at both the federal and state level. For example, if a municipal bond pays 2.75 percent annual interest, you would need to earn 5 percent on a taxable corporate bond to achieve the same after-tax return. To diversify, you can buy other states' municipal bonds as well. These nonresident state bonds are tax exempt at the federal level but not at the state level.

Step 5. Monitoring and Evaluation

Every portfolio needs care and maintenance over time, and the best way to make this process more effective and efficient is to use a tool. For example, the iRebal tool we use at Echo Wealth Management assigns each client's customized portfolio to a model that matches their risk number. From there, an advisor can set the criteria to alert them to rebalance the portfolio if the target percentage of each security exceeds a predetermined range. It's possible to set a minimum amount of buys or sells to avoid too many small trades. Your advisor can also incorporate your existing securities to set rules such as "exclude" or "don't sell" in addition to setting minimum cash balance for a specific account based on your withdrawal strategy. If you don't have this type of professional tool, use an Excel worksheet or other tools to monitor this closely. The models must be reviewed periodically to overweight or underweight certain asset classes based on market conditions and your worldview.

Without these cutting-edge tools, it would not be easy to monitor the risks of many accounts effectively and execute trades efficiently. For example, when stock markets declined sharply in December 2018,

Individual investors tend to have difficulty implementing disciplined and prudent investment strategies.

we were able to review portfolios for tax loss harvesting opportunities. Tax loss harvesting is the practice of selling a security that has experienced a loss on paper. By realizing, or "harvesting," a loss, investors are able to reduce current year's taxes by offsetting realized losses against both realized gains and income. The sold security is replaced by a similar one, maintaining an optimal asset allocation and expected returns.

Under the Wash Sale rule, if you sell a security for a loss and buy it back within thirty days before or after the loss-sale date, the loss cannot be immediately claimed for tax purposes. Therefore, to avoid violating the Wash Sale rule, make sure that you wait at least thirty days before buying back the security that you sold to realize losses across *all your accounts* including IRAs, even Roth IRAs. If you have accounts all over the place and managed by several advisors, it would be difficult to manage them to avoid the Wash Sale rule.

Individual investors tend to have difficulty implementing disciplined and prudent investment strategies, especially rebalancing, where it's necessary to sell the temporary winners and buy the temporary losers. However, this is an important part of monitoring and evaluating your investment plan. Rebalancing helps you avoid taking too much risk after the equity market performed well, and over time you are buying low and selling high.

Final Thoughts

Constructing your investment plan is a large undertaking. You must set your goals and prepare a solid financial plan first. You must figure out your risk tolerance and timeframe, construct your portfolio, implement your investment plan, locate assets, review your unrealized gains, correct your concentrated stock position, and continue to monitor and evaluate your portfolio. In order to do this effectively, here are five questions to ask yourself:

1. Have you updated your financial plan recently to reflect your current goals and resources?

2. Have you done an assessment of your risk number that can guide you in creating the right asset allocation for your situation?

3. What investment strategies do you have now, and how often do you evaluate them?

4. What changes would be required of you to take smart actions to generate better results for you and your family?

5. Could you achieve your financial goals sooner by surrounding yourself with smart, experienced, credible people who have your best interest at heart?

It's important to constantly reevaluate your overall strategy, not just the stocks within your portfolio, to make sure it's working for you in terms of your lifestyle and personal financial goals. Many people have unrealistic expectations of return on investment, which is made even more so when they don't understand their portfolios' risks and total costs (including internal fund expenses, advisory fees, and commissions). Individual investors tend to make emotional mistakes by selling the funds that lost value or firing their advisors at exactly the wrong time when stock markets experience a sharp decline.

Operating with a long-term perspective, we strive to avoid being reactive to market swings. Our belief is that if we haven't prepared for a sudden fluctuation, by the time it happens, it's too late to act in a meaningful way. We are committed to educating and coaching clients to promote an understanding of the value of having a longer time horizon.

This is why it's important to build a solid dream team and know what qualities to look for in each member. We'll look at this in more detail in the next chapter.

CHAPTER 7

Your Dream Team

Every great leader has an inner circle of friends, mentors, peers, mastermind partners, teachers, pupils, and family. These people comprise a team that in one way or another becomes part of their success. This means that to be successful at building and managing wealth, you need to assemble a dream team.

As you work to earn money and accumulate more savings and accounts, your financial life can become more complicated, especially if you also have a demanding job or a small business to run and a family to care for. You may feel you just don't have the time and energy to figure out the complex financial world to achieve your dreams and goals. Most people would rather plan family vacations than create their own financial plan and do investment research. Even for those who do plan, trying to take care of all its aspects is tough and may not be the best use of your precious time. The answer is the dream team. In this chapter, we'll look at the ideal dream team, who should be on it, and why they play an important role in your life.

Financial Planner

Your financial planner is your financial quarterback. He or she knows your overall financial picture, your money history, and your dreams and goals. When you are about to make an important financial decision, such as buying a home, retiring, or exercising your stock options, your financial planner is the first person to see. He or she should help you plan ahead, make sound investment decisions, and make sure all the members of your dream team are in alignment and meeting your needs.

While having a solid lineup of players on your team is essential, it's not a good idea to have more than one financial planner for two reasons: the first is that you'll end up paying more fees because most planners offer discounts based on the size of the portfolio under management; the second is that your investments are harder to monitor, which makes the combined risk harder to determine, especially when you need to make timely decisions. Think of it this way: you wouldn't go to one dentist to fix your upper teeth and go to another to fix your bottom teeth. Similarly, consolidating your accounts under one financial planner greatly simplifies your life, reduces costs, and makes your overall plan much easier to manage.

It's always a good idea to get recommendations from people you trust, such as your boss, CPAs, colleagues, or friends, to gain some insight into how a given financial planner/wealth manager works. There are three key attributes to look for in any financial planner, advisor, or wealth manager: trust and credibility, experience, and a growth mind-set.

Quick Guide to Financial Planners'/Investment Advisors' Accreditation

ACRONYM	FULL NAME	SUMMARY
	Emphasis on Financial Planning	
CFP®	Certified Financial Planner	Becoming the gold standard for financial planning.
CLU	Chartered Life Underwriter	Insurance-focused financial advice for estate planning.
CPA/PFS	Personal Financial Specialist	Issued by AICPA for the Certified Public Accountants who specialize in personal financial planning.
ChFC	Chartered Financial Consultant	Issued by American College of Financial Services. Not as hard to obtain as CFP®.
	Emphasis on Managing Investments	
CFA	Chartered Financial Analyst	Globally recognized for professional portfolio management, financial planning, and ethics. The gold standard for investment management.
CMT	Chartered Market Technician	Focusing on technical analysis, market research, and rules-based trading system design and testing.

TRUST AND CREDIBILITY

Titles and credentials may reflect the level of education and the breadth of professional service on which he or she is licensed to advise. For example, a chartered life underwriter (CLU) offers insurance, a certified public accountant (CPA) is licensed to provide accounting services, and a chartered financial analyst (CFA) charterholder is globally recognized for professional portfolio management. The CFA charter is a harder credential to obtain because it requires spending four to five years in study and the passing of three levels of exams. The credential also stipulates that he or she follows a fiduciary standard, which requires acting in the best interest of clients. This makes the CFA designation the gold standard for investment management.

For managing your investments and your overall wealth and lifestyle plan, a financial planner with Certified Financial Planner (CFP®) certification is the best option. You may also opt to work with a financial planner with the certified financial analyst (CFA) charter. The main difference between CFA charter and CFP® designation is that the latter focuses on overall financial plan including taxes, insurance, cash flow, retirement plan, investment plan, and estate plan, while a CFA's training focuses on deeper knowledge of statistics, economics, investment analysis, and portfolio building for both individuals and institutions such as insurance companies, mutual funds, banks, endowments, and

When hiring a financial planner, make sure that your service-level expectations are clear so that you can see if this partnership offers a good fit between what you are looking for and what the financial planner can and is willing to deliver.

foundations. Think of it this way: the CFP® certificate holders are family doctors, and CFA charter holders are specialists, such as neurosurgeons or cardiologists. If your financial planner does not have the CFA charter, it would be helpful if there is a CFA charter holder on the team either in house or outside the firm in order to offer more robust research into global economics and securities analysis to help build customized investment strategies.

It's important to know how fees are charged. Traditionally, financial planners were paid a commission on transactions and products they sold. In recent years, the Department of Labor has introduced new rules requiring financial planners to follow fiduciary standards in managing retirement accounts. Today, the financial planners with CFP® or CFA charter and some firms that adopted the CFP® Code of Ethics follow higher fiduciary standards than are traditionally found in the brokerage environment where brokers get paid on commission and the only requirement is that the product is suitable at the time of sale rather than in the long-term best interest of the client. Today, over 60 percent of planners in the United States are fee-based, meaning they charge an annual fee based on the account balance they manage rather than the products they sell.

When hiring a financial planner, make sure that your service-level expectations are clear so that you can see if this partnership offers a good fit between what you are looking for and what the financial planner can and is willing to deliver.

EXPERIENCE

The second quality to look for in a financial planner is experience. It's increasingly important today that you find someone who has a global perspective and uses a broad set of investment tools. It's helpful to look for someone who works with clients who have similar goals or face similar constraints as yours. This will allow you take full advantage of the planner's experience.

A GROWTH MIND-SET

A financial planner may have a lot of credentials and experience, but it's important that they have a growth mind-set and have processes in place to deliver consistent results. To know if your planner has a growth mind-set, pay attention to their willingness to actively seek new information, minimize biases, and routinely adapt their processes to grow your accounts. In addition, pay attention to how this planner utilizes his/her team and actively invests in continuing education by attending industry conferences and study groups.

You should also choose a planner with whom you feel comfortable discussing money issues and trust to act in your best interest. Your financial planner manages more than just finance; they should be able to guide you in financial training and in investment management.[28]

Tax Certified Public Accountant

Tax CPAs specialize in taxation. They are required to get 120 continuing education credits every three years to retain their credentials, so it's advisable that you work with a tax CPA who has an active license, as it means the continuing education criteria along with the ethics requirements have been met.

Some CPAs focus on individual tax returns, and some work on both individual and business tax returns, which means if you are a business owner, you need to make sure you work with a CPA who is proficient in both types of returns and is accountable and credible.

---

28 Visit www.plannersearch.org if you need help finding a financial planner that works well with you.

There are many reasons why the dream team of high-income and high-net-worth people should have CPAs to prepare their tax returns. First, tax laws are becoming more complicated, especially for high-income people. Second, your time is valuable, and preparing tax returns is time consuming. Doing research

Make sure that your trusted tax CPA works well with your financial planner. The tax CPA is the one who actually executes preparation of the tax returns, but the financial planner knows what is happening in every account.

and trying to stay on the top of tax law takes from the time you would rather spend doing things you love.

Make sure that your trusted tax CPA works well with your financial planner. The tax CPA is the one who actually executes preparation of the tax returns, but the financial planner knows what is happening in every account. When I have a new client, I always ask them about their relationship with their tax CPA and ask for an introduction so we can work as a team. Then, each tax season, with my client's approval, we organize their tax files, including tax forms such as 1099s, stock option exercise confirmations, stock donations to their donor-advised fund, and nondeductible IRA contributions. We then share them securely with their CPA. By working together in this way, your team can ensure you won't miss any opportunities to reduce taxes and keep more money in your pocket, while at the same time saving you valuable time and reducing stress throughout the year, especially during tax season.

If your financial planner doesn't ask for an introduction to your tax CPA, it would be a good idea to take a proactive step to introduce them and just make sure they collaborate well so you have less to worry about.

Estate Attorney

An estate attorney drafts legal documents, such as wills and trusts, healthcare directives, and financial powers of attorney. This person is a key player on your team, yet an astonishing number of people don't have estate plans in place.

If you don't have an estate attorney but have a trusted financial planner, ask the latter to introduce you to the former, and integrate both into your team. From there, your financial planner should be given a copy of your estate plan so that different scenarios can be run for different contingencies; for example, should you die tomorrow or twenty years from now.

If you do have an estate plan in place, make sure you're not making the common mistake of failing to implement it properly. For example, our client Mr. Gray paid several thousand dollars to an attorney years before he came to our firm to create a revocable living trust that dictated how his money should be managed during his lifetime and upon his death. The contents of this trust would have avoided probate, but none of his nonretirement account assets were moved into the trust because his former financial planner wasn't working in tandem with his legal advisor.

When looking for an estate attorney, ask one of your current trusted financial planners for a referral. Check the attorney's credentials online, and interview them to find out their specialty. For example, you don't want to hire a general business attorney to do your estate plan. When you interview them, ask them about the planning process, various available strategies, fees, who will implement your estate plan and how, and how frequently your plan is reviewed. This will help you avoid the problems Mr. Gray experienced when working with a disjointed team.

Independent Insurance Agents

An independent insurance agent, unlike a captive agent who works for a single company or sells the products of one company, is another key player on your dream team.

When looking for an independent insurance agent, it's important to find one who is licensed, trustworthy, and knowledgeable. Sometimes your financial planner may be able to fill this role if he/she has the proper licensing. For example, since I have a life and health insurance license registered in Minnesota, I can offer clients life insurance, disability insurance, and long-term-care insurance if necessary. I can help them shop for insurance by analyzing various companies' products before making recommendations. As I do not handle property and casualty insurance, I refer clients to an independent insurance agent who specializes in home, auto, and personal liability insurance, and we work together to protect their valuable assets.

If you choose not to get insurance through your financial planner, make sure you work with someone vetted by your financial planner. At the very least, make sure you work with someone with experience and knowledge who is not overselling you something you don't need. He or she should have many tools in the toolbox and is not just selling one or two products from a single company. There are a lot of not-so-competent insurance agents out there who just want to sell a product and get paid.

What you need on your team is someone who can work with the rest of your team and be willing and able to develop a long-term working relationship with you. A willingness to work with you and your team speaks volumes about the integrity of your insurance broker.

Other Team Members

While your financial planner, tax CPA, estate attorney, and insurance agent are important players on your team, it's important to make room for five more. Other team members should be your long-term-care specialist, college consultant, banker, or mortgage consultant. If you're a business owner, a bookkeeper should be on your team. As you age, your family doctor should be included, especially if you may develop or are developing dementia or other aging issues. Similarly, a trusted friend and a next-generation family member should also be on your team.

Having these players on your team can help you avoid some of the horror stories we hear of wealthy people being exploited in their declining years. Safeguarding against this is also part of your financial plan and part of the responsibility of your team.

For example, one elderly woman who had lived happily on a $6,000 monthly withdrawal from her investment account called her planner one day and said she needed $30,000. Her lifestyle hadn't changed, so this was unusual. Later, it was learned that she was being pressured by one of the daughters who was taking care of her to bail her out of a bad financial condition. It almost drained her portfolio. Without a complete and integrated team, no one noticed that she was being exploited and abused.

Make sure you have a discussion with your financial planner about what to do in the event of diminished mental capacity; that is, if it appears that you are not behaving in a rational way, or are losing the mental capacity to understand or be understood on the phone or in face-to-face meetings, or are forgetting things that you normally don't. It's a good idea to have a written plan in place with your financial planner that includes other team members and friends and family with whom he or she should talk. It's a good idea to sign a letter to authorize your financial planner to contact these trusted personal and professional contacts. With this contingency in place, your team can help you avoid being exploited in the event of diminished mental and physical capacity.

Final Thoughts

Your team is not only essential to owning your financial future; it's also essential to owning your future long into your declining years when you may have diminished capacity and need not only a trusted friend but also a financial quarterback you can count on.

Make sure you put enough thought into forming your team and introducing them to each other. When thinking about your team, ask yourself:

1. Who are your most trusted professionals?

2. Have you taken steps to introduce your financial planner to the other key professionals in your circle so that they can collaborate to serve you?

3. Are your team members experienced and equipped to maximize your wealth opportunities and support your lifestyle?

4. Who are your closest friends?

5. Do you have a plan to make yourself bulletproof against fraud and elder abuse?

Now that you know how to build your team and what to look for in each member, we'll turn to each of these areas in the next chapters in more detail and examine what each team player should be bringing to the table to serve you.

CHAPTER 8

Tax Strategies

Just as diversification is important in investing, income source diversification is also important when it comes to planning for your financial future. While today's top income rate of 37 percent is relatively low compared to historical income tax rates, which were as high as 94 percent during World War II, it's still vitally important that you diversify your income sources in order to have more flexibility in dealing with potential future tax increases.

The US progressive tax system ensures that all taxpayers pay the same rates on the same levels of taxable income. The overall effect is that people with higher incomes pay higher taxes. For tax planning, you need to understand the difference between your marginal tax rate and your effective, or average tax rate. Your marginal tax rate, or tax bracket, is not the tax rate you pay on all of your income after adjustments and deductions. It's applied to your additional income over a certain threshold amount. Your effective tax rate is the total taxes you pay divided by your taxable income. Effective tax rate only matters as a group of taxpayers is compared to another group of taxpayers to illustrate how much taxes each group pays based on their income levels. For individual tax planning, your focus should be on your marginal tax rate because you can take some actions to reduce taxes by not getting into the next higher tax bracket.

How Tax Brackets Work

What if your taxable income is $78,950?

Married filing jointly in 2019 puts you in the 12% tax bracket, but this doesn't mean you pay 12% on all your income.

Here is the math:

First tax bracket: $19,400 x 10% =	$1,940
Second tax bracket: ($78,950 - $19,400) x 12% =	$7,146
Total Federal Income Tax:	$9,086

This tax table shows a 12% marginal tax rate, but an effective tax rate of 11.51%.

What if your taxable income is $321,450?

If married filing jointly in 2019, you will be in the 24% tax bracket.

Here is the math:

First tax bracket: $19,400 x 10% =	$1,940
Second tax bracket: ($78,950 - $19,400) x 12% =	$7,146
Third tax bracket: ($168,400 - $78,950) x 22% =	$19,679
Fourth tax bracket: ($321,450 - $168,400) x 24% =	$36,732
Total Federal Income Tax:	$65,497

This tax table shows a marginal tax rate of 24%, but an effective tax rate of 20.38%.

Some people think if they earn more money, all of their income becomes subject to the next-highest tax bracket. They think they will pay more taxes and possibly have less money left over than they would have had they earned less. As you can see from these examples, that is not true. Each dollar you earn only affects the tax rate and taxes owed on additional income and not to the *Rates are not the only factor in your final tax bill. Some tax benefits phase out at higher income levels. In some tax scenarios, it may make sense to avoid higher tax brackets if possible.*

dollars earned in lower tax brackets. You always have more money after taxes when you earn more, even after paying additional taxes at a higher tax rate. However, rates are not the only factor in your final tax bill. Some tax benefits phase out at higher income levels. In some tax scenarios, it may make sense to avoid higher tax brackets if possible.

Eight Tax Strategies

Now that you know how the progressive tax system works, here are eight strategies that you can adopt to maximize tax savings.

STRATEGY 1: DIVERSIFY YOUR INCOME SOURCES

Since you cannot predict your future income tax rates, owning investments in all three tax buckets gives you the flexibility you need to reduce taxes.

Many people miss out on opportunities to save taxes by failing to realize that they are making tax-inefficient decisions and by failing to own investments in all three tax buckets: tax deferred (401(k) and IRA), tax-free (Roth IRA and HSA), and taxable (individual, joint, revocable living trust). These three buckets provide different opportunities: by maximizing your after-tax-rate return, you pay only the taxes that you are required to pay, you can reduce your tax bill, and you can position yourself better for the long term.

A taxable traditional IRA withdrawal is taxed at the highest ordinary income tax rate. People often forget how much the financial climate can change. For example, a higher income earner could find himself/herself with a tax hike down the road if the government finds itself in need of money. Someone with $2 million invested for retirement could suddenly find their picture changing due to a future change in tax laws that raise ordinary income tax rates. However, if you have a Roth IRA, you may be able to withdraw some money from this account (since you use after-tax dollars to fund a Roth IRA, taxes are not paid on Roth IRA withdrawals) instead of your traditional IRA to lower taxable income. This will allow you pay taxes at a lower rate. If tax rates go down later, you can switch back to withdrawing from your IRA and taxable accounts.

Before 2010, only taxpayers who earned an adjusted gross income of less than $100,000 were allowed to convert any IRA balance to a Roth IRA. Since 2010, the IRS has allowed any individuals to convert their traditional IRA to Roth IRA regardless of income level. This change in tax laws has created the "back door Roth" strategy. High-income people now can contribute to their IRAs but have these treated as nondeductible IRA contributions on their tax returns. This does not reduce the current tax bill for high-income people, but it will help later when Roth conversion happens.

For example, the non-deductible IRA contribution amount (maximum $6,000 for people younger than fifty in 2019) is the cost basis in the IRS system. If you don't have any pretax dollars (i.e., rollover from your old 401(k)) in this IRA or any IRA accounts under your social security number, and if the balance grows to $7,000 in a year, you can choose to convert the entire account balance of $7,000 from an IRA to your Roth IRA by paying ordinary income taxes on the profit of $1,000. The $7,000 in this Roth IRA can grow and all distributions after age 59.5 will be tax free. You can contribute to an IRA as long as you have earned income and before age 70.5. The goal of the "back door Roth" strategy is to increase the size of your tax-free bucket without paying too much in taxes now because Congress may increase tax rates, and when the current tax cut expires on December 31, 2025, converting your IRA money to Roth IRA may be subject to higher tax rates.

For a more affluent married couple who are projected to be in a 32+ percent marginal tax bracket in the future when RMDs (required minimum distribution based on life expectancy and IRA balance) begin at age 70.5, it is a good idea to convert some IRA money to Roth IRA money for the next few years in order to fill up in the low tax brackets by paying no more than 24 percent federal marginal tax rate (staying below taxable income of $321,450 for married filing jointly). Thus, the decision to pay taxes at today's rates can generate potential tax benefits in the long term.

People often overlook the importance of having a Roth IRA account. Because Roth IRA contributions do not reduce their current tax bill, they may not see the benefits of putting a small amount in a Roth IRA and leaving it to grow for twenty or thirty years. At retirement, if you find yourself in a 55 percent tax bracket because the political climate has changed and with it the tax laws, having a tax-free account will offer you a lot of flexibility. You can treat the taxes you choose to pay now on the Roth conversion as "tax insurance" because it helps to manage the risk relating to potential future tax rate increase.

You can also consider switching from contributions to your traditional 401(k) to Roth 401(k) if your employer also offers a Roth 401(k). You can contribute some to the traditional 401(k) plan with pretax dollars and some to the Roth 401(k) plan with after-tax dollars as long as the total does not exceed the IRS maximum per year. In this way, you can essentially increase your retirement savings by funding it with after-tax dollars and distributions from Roth 401(k) plans that will be tax-free after age 59.5.

There are other advantages to having a Roth IRA: you are able to make contributions at any age even after age seventy as long as you and/or your spouse have earned income; you are not required to take a required minimum distribution (RMD) from a Roth IRA when you turn age 70.5; a nonworking spouse can open a Roth IRA based on the working spouse's earnings if they file tax returns jointly; you can still make your annual contributions if you convert money from a traditional IRA to a Roth IRA in the same year; and you can contribute to a Roth IRA even if you participate in a retirement plan through your employer. There are, however, income limitations for eligibility of Roth contributions if you are eligible to participate in a retirement plan through your employer.

The Roth IRA allows you to pay taxes now at a certain rate instead of paying taxes later at an uncertain rate. This is a great way to hedge against future income tax increases. Use some financial planning tools to project your future marginal tax bracket based on your projected taxable income year by year to age ninety-five, and use today's tax laws to help you make smart decisions.

STRATEGY 2: HELP YOUR CHILDREN FUND THEIR ROTH IRAS

Many people are more concerned about their children than themselves. They see a terrible job market, insecure jobs, or a lack of full employment. Their children aren't getting the jobs for which they went to college. They have student loans. In today's economy, children often don't have a great financial foundation or an understanding of basic financial planning. Therefore,

The Roth IRA allows you to pay taxes now at a certain rate instead of paying taxes later at an uncertain rate. This is a great way to hedge against future income tax increases.

many people are asking: Is there something we can do to help out our children in the long term and into retirement?

If your children have part-time or summer jobs, you should encourage them to open a Roth IRA and then help them fund up to a maximum contribution of $6,000 for the year 2019. Even if they only make $4,000 per year and save $2,000 for their Roth IRA, you can match that with another $2,000. Those starting out in their career should also contribute enough to their 401(k) plan to get the benefit of their employer's full match.

If the employer matches fifty cents to a dollar of contribution up to 6 percent of compensation, your child must contribute at least 6 percent of his or her pay in order to receive the full match (i.e., 3 percent of his or her pay). This gives a 100 percent return on his or her investments without much risk. When they are starting out in their career, generally it is better to contribute to a Roth 401(k) than a traditional pretax 401(k), as their income is likely to increase in the future. This will encourage them to start saving now and invest early for their retirement.

The long-term growth of these tax-free retirement accounts is significant because they can leave it there for fifty years. This comes back to the idea of meticulous planning: by accumulating small amounts consistently over time, even a 5–6 percent rate of return compounded over fifty years will become a big account.

STRATEGY 3: BE CREATIVE WITH CHARITABLE GIVING

If you have any appreciated stocks in your nonretirement accounts, instead of writing checks to charities or using payroll deductions at work, you can choose to donate the appreciated securities that you have held for at least one year to the charities. You can deduct the market value of the securities on the date of gifting as a charitable deduction. This is a better way than paying taxes on the realized capital gains when you sell them and then writing checks to the charities.

If you want to have a major charitable deduction to lower your taxable income in one year but are uncertain about which charities and how much you want to give each year in the future, you can consider setting up a donor-advised fund through your financial advisor and transfer the appreciated securities on which you have unrealized long-term gains and deduct the fair market value as a charitable deduction on your tax returns in the year you fund the donor-advised fund. You don't have to determine the recipients of your generosity until later years.

For example, if you normally give $5,000 to charities by writing checks, you can donate a total of $100,000 of appreciated securities (with a cost basis of $60,000) to your donor-advised fund, and you can save about about $45,000 in income taxes if you pay a total of 45 percent federal and state income tax this year. When you sell the securities to diversify to other investments inside the account, you don't have to report the long-term gains of $40,000 on your tax returns. This will save you an additional $13,460 in long-term capital gains tax (Federal 20%, 3.8% net investment income tax, and state 9.85%). If this account grows, you will have more money to help charities. You do not take another charitable deduction when the money (grant) goes to charities from this account. Upon your death, the successors you have named will continue your legacy.

A charitable remainder trust can avoid capital gains taxes on appreciated assets, allowing you to receive income for life and receive a tax deduction now for a charitable contribution that will be made after your death. A charitable lead trust can avoid taxes on appreciated assets, earn an immediate tax deduction, and still provide an inheritance for your heirs later. Charitable trusts are complex vehicles most often used in specific situations like possession of ultralow-cost basis stock or properties.

STRATEGY 4: OPEN A HEALTH SAVINGS ACCOUNT

A health savings account (HSA) is an important part of any tax diversification strategy. Studies show that a sixty-five-year-old couple will need $245,000 to cover health care expenses in retirement.[29] Think of your retirement savings (IRAs and 401(k)) as going to pay for other retirement expenses such as food, shelter, and clothes, and you can see that you need to jump-start saving in your HSA for your health care costs (including Medicare premiums) in retirement.

An HSA can be a powerful tool to help you save and invest now and then pay for your qualified medical expenses during retirement. It also offers triple tax benefits. First, contributions are made with pretax dollars through payroll if your employer offers it. If not, you can purchase a high deductible health plan (HDHP) on your own in the insurance market, set up your own HSA online, and make contributions before the tax return filing deadline. Distributions

29 Ashlea Ebeling, "Fidelity's Retiree Health Care Cost Estimate Rises To $245,000 A Couple," *Forbes* (October 7, 2015). Available at https://www.forbes.com/sites/ashleaebeling/2015/10/07/fidelitys-retiree-health-care-cost-estimate-rises-to-245000-a-couple/#39e79727181b.

Think of your retirement savings (IRAs and 401(k)) as going to pay for other retirement expenses such as food, shelter, and clothes, and you can see that you need to jump-start saving in your HSA for your health care costs (including Medicare premiums) in retirement.

are income-tax-free if you use them to pay for qualified medical expenses. Typical retiree expenses on health care are often as high as $500/month, much of which are HSA-eligible qualified medical expenses.

An HSA balance doesn't expire; unlike **a Flexible Spending Account (FSA)**, you don't need to spend the balance within the calendar year. As long as your medical expenses aren't reported on tax returns, you can be reimbursed from your HSA many years from now. The benefit for high-income earners is that they should get tax benefits from contributions to an HSA instead of claiming medical expenses on their tax return (Schedule A). This is beneficial because they are unlikely to receive any tax benefits since total qualified medical expenses for the calendar year must exceed 10 percent of adjusted gross income starting in 2019. It is a good idea to set aside extra cash in your savings account to pay for nondeductible medical expenses (i.e., $5,000) instead of taking distributions immediately from your HSA. This allows the HSA balance to be invested for growth, which will help offset inevitably higher medical expenses during retirement. Unlike an IRA, the HSA balance can also be distributed before age 59.5 without incurring taxes and penalties.

You can contribute up to $3,500 a year if you have an individual HDHP or $7,000 if you have a family HDHP, with an additional $1,000 if you are fifty-five or older. However, it's important not to exceed the maximum contributions set by IRS, particularly since excess contributions aren't deductible. You will end up paying a 6 percent excise tax on excess contributions unless you withdraw the excess contributions by the due date of your tax return for the year the contributions were made. If you and your spouse each have a separate high deductible health insurance plan through your employers, make sure you coordinate your contribution amounts so that your total contributions as a family plus employers' matching does not exceed the annual maximum.

For every dollar you put in, you get a tax benefit. If you don't use the money in your account, it can grow, and you don't pay taxes on this growth. When you do withdraw the money, as long as you are using it to pay for qualified medical expenses, the money remains tax-free.

STRATEGY 5: USING MUNICIPAL BONDS

If you are a high-income earner, incorporating municipal bonds into your taxable accounts may be a good tax strategy. When your portfolio construction calls for some fixed income allocation for the purpose of diversification to reduce risks, various bonds, such as high-yield bonds, corporate bonds, and government bonds, can be purchased in your IRA account because the interest income is not reported on tax returns each year. Remember, you only have to report income from an IRA when it is distributed out of an IRA to you.

If you buy the municipal bonds in your resident state, interest is tax-free at both the federal and state level. If you buy municipal bonds in other states, you still receive tax-free income at the federal level; that is, if your federal income tax bracket is 35 percent and the Minnesota tax bracket is 9.85 percent, your combined tax bracket is 44.85 percent. For example, an investment-grade municipal bond in Minnesota that matures on February 1, 2030, and pays 3 percent annual interest is equivalent to a corporate bond that pays 5.44 percent. The math for tax equivalent rate: 3 percent is divided by (1 minus 0.4485) = 5.44 percent. If you cannot find the similar credit rating and maturity date corporate bonds that pay as high as 5.44 percent, then consider buying municipal bonds to receive tax-free income inside your taxable account (joint, individual, or revocable trust account).

STRATEGY 6: NET UNREALIZED APPRECIATION STRATEGY

Before the Enron crisis, many employers matched company stock in employees' 401(k) plans, and employees kept that stock for many years. As they retired and considered taking distributions from their 401(k), they had to decide what to do with the employer stock. Before deciding to sell the stock inside the plan and rolling over the entire balance to an IRA, an analysis of cost basis and tax situation should be completed. If the stock's cost basis (the original purchase price) is low and in the region of 20 percent to 30 percent of the current market value, it may make sense to transfer the shares to a taxable brokerage account (such as joint, individual or revocable trust account, but not an IRA account). You would pay ordinary income tax on the *cost basis only* in the year of taking the stock out of the 401(k) plan. Any appreciation above the cost basis is treated as long-term capital gains when you sell the shares inside your taxable brokerage account. The mutual funds inside your 401(k) could be sold, and *the entire balance must be rolled over into an IRA in the same calendar year as you take the stock out of the plan.* The benefit is to pay long term capital gains tax (maximum 20 percent, lower than the ordinary income tax rate) on a substantial portion of the appreciation.

In December 2018, my client Mary's father passed away suddenly at age eighty, and her mother, Susan (age seventy-nine), inherited a large 401(k) plan balance with about 40 percent in employer stock. The cost basis was about 20 percent of market value. I reviewed the most recent 401(k) statement on December 14 and learned that the required minimum distribution (RMD) for the year 2018 was about $50,000. This needed to be taken out immediately to avoid a 50 percent tax penalty assessed by IRS. After analyzing her other assets, Social Security income, and pension income to calculate her projected tax rate in the future along with her estimated living expenses, it became apparent that taking out this employer stock in-kind and paying income taxes on the $75,000 cost basis was the best choice for her because this distribution of stock met the RMD requirement for the year. She would have over $350,000 worth of stock in a taxable account on which she would potentially pay lower long-term capital gain taxes on the appreciation above $75,000 cost basis when sold at a later time. This timely action before the end of the year resulted in an immediate savings of $25,000 in IRS penalties and gave her peace of mind. After a late night just before Christmas of research, analysis, and several conference calls with the retirement plan and transfer agent, I was excited about the positive result! A lesson for the reader: never wait until the second half of the year to take the RMD, as it may take a few months for the beneficiary to figure out how to take the RMD in a timely fashion.

Because she also inherited the same employer stock in her other taxable brokerage accounts in which she received a stepped-up basis (the cost basis is now the market value on the date of his death), it was best to sell the shares with a higher cost basis first in order to diversify but keep the shares (low basis that came out of the 401(k) plan) for the longer term. When she passes away with this low-cost-basis stock, her children will inherit this stock with stepped-up basis so that they don't pay any taxes if sold.

This strategy, which involves the net unrealized appreciation (NUA) of employer stock inside a retirement plan, doesn't apply to everyone, but it's a good idea to investigate if you or your spouse has low-cost-basis employer stock inside a retirement plan.

STRATEGY 7: MANAGE TAX BRACKET AND HARVEST GAIN

Long-term capital gains generally have preferential tax rates rather than ordinary income tax rates. A recent tax cut offered a series of tiered preferential rates, from 0 percent for those in the lowest tax brackets, to 15 percent for those in the middle, and 20 percent (plus 3.8 percent net investment income tax if AGI for a married couple filing jointly is greater than $250,000) for the highest-income taxpayers (still a good deal for someone who is at the 37 percent top tax rate on ordinary income). Unlike tax-loss harvesting, which helps lower your income tax bill by selling investments that are currently trading for less than their purchase price and then using those losses to offset other capital gains or reduce taxable income, capital gains harvesting is a strategy by which you can turn unrealized long-term capital gains into realized capital gains by paying taxes at a lower rate now if you expect your tax rates to go up in the future. The Tax Cuts and Jobs Act (TCJA) will "sunset" and change to the higher tax rates and lower standard deduction as of 2017 if Congress does not change them by December 31, 2025.

When you convert the money in your IRA to a Roth IRA, you pay ordinary income tax, not the capital gain tax rate. When you sell appreciated securities that you have held for at least one year inside your taxable accounts, the realized long-term gains are subject to the capital gains tax rates. Capital gains rates have their own brackets that differ from ordinary income tax rates, and good tax planning lies in capturing the 0 percent and 15 percent capital gains tax rates.

Determining The Marginal Tax Rate For Various Types Of Income In 2019

Individual income above...	Couple's income above...	Income "type"	Ordinary Income	L/T gains & qual. dividends	Pass-Thru Business Deduction	Wage earned income	Self-employed income	Net inv. income	AMT rate	AMT exemption phaseout
$0	$0	Taxable	10%		-2%					
$9,700	$19,400	Taxable	12%	0%	-2.4%					
$39,375	$78,750	Taxable				7.65%	15.30%			
$39,475	$78,950	Taxable	22%		-4.4%				26%	
N/A	$132,900	Earned				7.65% / 1.45%	15.3% / 2.9%			
$84,200	$168,400	Taxable	24%		-4.8%			0%		
$132,900	N/A	Earned				1.45%	2.90%			
$160,725	N/A	Taxable	32% / 24%		Up to 29% / -4.8%					
$194,800	$194,800	AMTI		15%						
$200,000	$250,000	Earned				2.35%	3.80%			0%
$200,000	$250,000	AGI						3.80%		
$204,100	N/A	Taxable	35% / 24%		0% / Up to 29%					
$210,700	N/A	Taxable	35% / 32%							
N/A	$321,450	Taxable							28%	
N/A	$408,200	Taxable								
N/A	$421,400	Taxable	35%							
$434,550	$488,850	Taxable								
$510,300	N/A	AMTI			0%					
$510,300	$612,350	Taxable	37.0%	20%						
$797,100	N/A	AMTI								7% / 0%
N/A	$1,020,600	AMTI								0%
N/A	$1,467,400	AMTI								0% / 7%

Source: Michael Kitces (www.kitces.com)

It is best to work with a qualified tax advisor to analyze your various income sources, including distributions from your IRA, interest income, and long-term capital gains. I'm going to provide the general considerations on the *order* of when to do partial Roth conversion and when to realize long-term capital gains when selling appreciated securities inside your taxable accounts:

1. For people who have negative taxable income (i.e., deductions exceed income), partial Roth conversions will effectively have a marginal tax rate of 0 percent at the federal level. Therefore, absorbing any negative taxable income with a partial Roth conversion should come first.

2. From there, it's hard to beat 0 percent on the long-term capital gains rate by realizing some long-term capital gains in your taxable accounts.

3. Once the 0 percent long-term capital gains bracket is filled up, for those households that already have too much in Social Security benefits, pensions, passive income, RMDs, or other income sources, and are no longer exposed to the AMT, it may be more beneficial to conduct partial Roth conversions by paying the 22 percent or even 24 percent tax rate, to avoid the 32+ percent brackets.

4. In the most extreme cases, for people who will always be at the top tax brackets (over $612,350 taxable income for future years), it may be advisable to harvest partial Roth conversions at 32 percent or 35 percent tax brackets to avoid the very top (37 percent) tax bracket in the future. This can be done while avoiding paying the top capital gains tax rate, which is reached at $434,550 of income for individuals and $488,850 for married couples.

STRATEGY 8: MANAGE DEDUCTIONS

In 2017, the standard deduction was increased. Today, only 15 percent of people benefit from itemized deductions because the standard deduction is actually higher than their itemized deduction. For example, a retired couple that no longer has mortgage interest to deduct loses a big component of itemized deductions. If they give $5,000 to charity each year, this still does not put them over the $27,000 (if over age 65 in 2019) standard deduction for a married couple.

In addition, in 2019, the tax law changed again so that state income tax and property tax, which used to be unlimited, is now capped at $10,000 a year. A retired couple whose property tax and charitable giving only amounts to $15,000 falls far below the standard deduction for married couples. However, they can use a donor-advised fund to maximize their deductions. For example, if they have stocks in Apple and Ecolab that have a substantial unrealized long-term gain, they can put $50,000 in a donor-advised fund. This can be added to their $10,000 property tax deduction to give them an itemized deduction of $60,000 in that year. This is significantly more than the $27,000 standard deduction and will result in a large tax savings (about $11,550 based on a 35 percent combined tax bracket) in the current year. In the following years, if they decide to grant the money inside the donor-advised fund to the charity, they can return to using the standard deduction. Bunching their giving into one year can save them thousands of dollars overall.

Another strategy for tax savings to benefit the family involves contributing to a college savings 529 plan, which produces some state income tax savings and funding for the future qualified education costs of a loved one. Recent tax law changes mean you can also use this fund to pay for private elementary, middle, or high school up to

$10,000 per person per year. These contributions do not reduce your tax bill much today, but all distributions from 529 plans to pay for qualified education expenses are income-tax-free regardless of your income level. Some states including Minnesota allow taxpayers to deduct the 529 plan contributions on their state income tax returns.

Final Thoughts

Tax planning is not just for tax season. You don't do some planning and forget about it. It's important to think about tax planning in the same way you think about investing. The idea of meticulous planning, building on this plan, creating an investment strategy, and executing and monitoring it also applies to tax planning. This is particularly important when there are major changes in tax laws.

Ask yourself what type of tax planning you have done this year with the tax CPA on your dream team. If you don't have a tax CPA on your team, you'll need to have basic knowledge and keep up with tax laws so as to not overpay your taxes. Second, ask yourself what your federal marginal tax rate was last year, and identify how much more taxable income you can earn before you reach your next tax bracket. Review and identify two actions you can take now to potentially improve your tax situation next year and into the future.

Remember, tax planning is not only for April. It means all-year-round planning and even multiyear tax planning using projection tools. It's never a good idea to wait until the eleventh hour to try to implement long-term tax strategies.

CHAPTER 9

Estate Planning

Mr. and Mrs. Gold, new clients, came to me to create a retirement plan a few years ago. During our discovery meeting, I realized that their estate plan had been prepared fifteen years earlier in Illinois and had not been updated since, despite them owning property in Wisconsin and living in and hoping to retire in Minnesota. Fifteen years earlier, Mr. Gold had put a trust in place, but no assets were placed in the trust after it was created by the estate attorney because his financial planner wasn't working in tandem with his legal advisor. Nor had Mr. Gold changed his individual accounts to a revocable living trust (an entity that is formed to dictate how money in the trust should be managed during his lifetime and upon death) to hold his investments. Furthermore, the beneficiary forms for retirement accounts and insurance policies hadn't been updated. In short, Mr. Gold had made almost all of the six most common mistakes people make when it comes to estate planning.

This chapter will offer some basic knowledge of estate planning documents and advice on how to go about working with an estate attorney and your financial planner to plan ahead so that you don't inadvertently make any of Mr. Gold's mistakes.

What Is Estate Planning?

Estate planning is the systematic approach to organizing your personal and financial affairs in order to deal with the possibility of mental incapacity and the certainty of death.

Mortality is not a subject on which most people want to focus, but without a proper estate plan to address issues relating to mental or physical incapacity and death, you could give your loved ones unneeded headaches and unnecessary costs relating to handling your estate.

An adequate estate plan must ensure that your assets are properly used to support you during life, ensure that your remaining assets are distributed according to your wishes at death, and must be structured so that you can implement your plan in order to minimize fees, costs, and taxes. Depending on the size of your estate and personal situation, estate planning will generally follow either a will-based plan or trust-based plan approach.

> *Without a proper estate plan to address issues relating to mental or physical incapacity and death, you could give your loved ones unneeded headaches and unnecessary costs relating to handling your estate.*

A will-based plan tells the probate court how you want your assets distributed after your death. It names whom you want to have your assets pass to and how you want them distributed. Since the probate court oversees the process, it is open to the public. A trust-based plan includes a revocable living trust and is suitable for high-net-worth individuals and those who want privacy and more control over how their assets are distributed. This trust holds the title to your assets during your lifetime and transfers them to your named beneficiaries upon your death outside the probate process. This plan requires more up-front work, but if you are a high-net-worth individual, it can help you reduce estate administration costs, provide privacy, and potentially lower your tax liability after your death.

Let us look at each type of plan in more detail.

Will-Based Estate Planning

Depending on your current family and financial situations, will-based estate planning will include three essential legal estate planning documents[30]: last will and testament, health care directive, and durable power of attorney. The laws of your state may dictate the need for other estate planning documents. If this is the case, your estate attorney will be able to assist you in preparing all of the estate planning documents that you will need.

LAST WILL AND TESTAMENT

Your last will and testament, or simply your will, is a legal document that ensures that your money, property, and personal belongings will be distributed as you wish after your death.

The law doesn't require that you have a will, but if you die without one, your resident state will divide your property based on state laws (called "intestacy"). If you have a spouse and children, the

---

30 These are the names of Minnesota legal documents. Other states may use different names.

property will go to them by a set formula; if not, the property will descend in the following order: grandchildren, parents, brothers and sisters, or more distant relatives. If you want to leave a property to a friend or a charity, you will definitely need a will. You also need a will if you want to prevent someone from inheriting some of your money.

You can name a guardian for your minor children in your will. This guardian must be someone over eighteen who is willing to assume the responsibility. It's a huge responsibility, so make sure you talk to the potential guardian before naming him or her, and share with them any wishes you have for your children after you die (for example, living in your city or moving someplace else).

Your will also names a personal representative, also known as an executor or administrator. This person oversees payment of your debt and distribution of your assets according to your will. A personal representative is considered a fiduciary and must observe a high standard of care when dealing with your estate. Most people choose their spouse and adult child or relative, a friend, a trust company, or an attorney to fulfill this duty, but any competent adult can be named a personal representative in a will. Since your personal representative will handle your assets, you should always pick someone you trust.

Your personal representative is responsible for starting the probate process and filing tax returns. Probate is the legal process of settling your estate in court after you die. The process begins by filing an application or petition with the probate court and ends when all debts and taxes are paid and all assets are distributed. During the process, your property is gathered and inventoried, your debts are paid, and everything left over is divided among your beneficiaries. The need for probate depends on the amount of property you own, the type of property you own, and whether you own alone or with others. If there is disagreement over your will, a probate judge will resolve the differences.

If you have property in another state, your representative will need to go through the probate process in that state if the property is not held in a trust. We'll talk about trusts later.

The federal estate and gift tax exemption amount is currently $11.4 million per person in 2019, but each state has its own estate tax exemption. In Minnesota, it's $2.7 million per person for 2019 and $3 million for 2020 and after. If your gross estate is less than that, your estate does not need to file an estate tax return. Make sure you check the tax laws in your state.

Some items are not subject to probate, including property owned as joint tenants, jointly held bank accounts, payable-on-death accounts, transfer-on-death accounts, life insurance proceeds to a specific beneficiary, and pension benefits with a designated beneficiary in the event you die. Transfers between spouses are generally not taxable due to marital exemption but may need to go through probate if the account is an individual account instead of joint account or trust account. For example, if you are survived by your spouse, he or she will take the title to your home along with any jointly owned bank or brokerage accounts or retirement accounts (if your spouse is the primary beneficiary) without owing any estate taxes on the estate or going through the probate courts if your estate is below the estate tax exemption amount.

For any beneficiaries, brokerage firms, such as TD Ameritrade, allow you to add a payable-on-death instruction on the individual account so that you can name your beneficiary without having to go through probate. Naming beneficiaries on your individual accounts is therefore a simple tool that helps you get your money to the people you want more quickly. The same applies to life insurance; the designated beneficiary gets the death benefits. You can also name your revocable trust to obtain the same result.

Remember, the designated beneficiary on an insurance policy supersedes the will. In other words, he or she will get the death benefits regardless of who you name in your will. Therefore, make sure the beneficiary designation form actually matches your wishes, and talk to your estate attorney and/or financial planner to make sure your assets are properly organized, titled, and designated in the event of your death.

A new client who is a recent widow came to see me this year, and her deceased husband had named her and her two minor children as equal beneficiaries of his life insurance policy. He made a mistake because minors cannot take control of the inheritance until reaching the age of majority—eighteen in many states, but sometimes twenty-one. Even though she was appointed as the conservator for her minor children after an attorney was hired to file a petition, she still has to follow all the tedious rules to manage the two conservatorship accounts and track expenses separately in order to file reports timely ongoing until they turn age eighteen. Her children will receive 100 percent control over the accounts when they turn age eighteen, according to Minnesota law.

To avoid these kinds of hassles, he could have named his spouse as primary beneficiary and a trust for the benefit of minor children as the contingent beneficiary. If the parent creates a trust, the trustee will manage the inherited asset for the minor. This is often the best method because the parents can specify the age or ages at which their children will get control of their trust assets, which usually is later than eighteen.

HEALTH CARE DIRECTIVE

A health care directive, sometimes called a living will and power of attorney for health care, is a written document that informs others of your health care wishes. It allows you to name a person (or "agent") to make decisions for you if you are unable to do so. In most states, anyone eighteen or older can make a health care directive.

A health care directive is useful if you become unable to adequately communicate your health care wishes. The directive guides your physician, family, and friends regarding your care at a time when you are not able to provide that information. While you will still receive medical care without a health care directive, it will help you get exactly the care you would like, particularly near the end of your life when your interests may not be the same as those who survive you.

Before doing a health care directive, think about your goals, values, and preferences about health care, such as the type of treatment you do or do not want—for example, intubation or the use of feeding tubes. You should also consider whether you want to donate organs, tissues, or body parts. You can also include wishes for funeral arrangements.

A health care directive can be general or specific, but you should include the following information:

1. The name of the person(s) you designate as your agent or joint agents to make health care decisions for you and alternate agents in case the first agent is unavailable.

2. Directions to joint agents, if assigned, regarding the process or standards by which they are to reach a health care decision.

3. Your goals, values, and preferences about health care.

4. The types of medical treatment you want or do not want,

including instructions about artificial nutrition and hydration.

5. How you want your agent(s) to make decisions.

6. Where you want to receive care.

7. Your preferences regarding mental health treatments, including those that are intrusive through use of electro-shock therapy or neuroleptic medications.

8. Your desire to donate organs, tissues, or other body parts.

9. Your funeral arrangements (for example, burial or cremation).

Take the time to make your document personal so that it reflects your wishes. Give a copy to your health care agent, and keep a copy handy at home and at work.

DURABLE POWER OF ATTORNEY

A power of attorney form is a document in which you authorize somebody to act on your behalf regarding financial decisions. This person is known as the attorney-in-fact. You can determine how much power the person will have over your financial affairs.

A "durable" power of attorney form is one that remains valid even if you become incompetent or incapacitated. You can design it to take effect immediately or stipulate that it only goes into effect when you become unable to make decisions for yourself. This is known as a "springing power of attorney."

You can choose to give your attorney-in-fact power to do some or all of the following:

1. Use your assets to pay your everyday expenses and those of your family.

2. Buy, sell, maintain, mortgage, or pay taxes on real estate and other property.

3. Manage benefits from Social Security, Medicare, or other government programs, or civil or military service.

4. Invest your money in stocks, bonds, and mutual funds.

5. Handle transactions with your bank and other financial institutions.

6. Buy and sell insurance policies and annuities for you.

7. File and pay your taxes.

8. Operate your small business.

9. Claim property you inherit or are otherwise entitled to.

10. Hire someone to represent you in court.

11. Manage your retirement accounts.

Therefore, it's important that when you are not able to make financial decisions for yourself, you decide specifically who should make these decisions for you.

Having these three documents in place ensures your wishes are carried out while you are alive, should you become incapacitated, and after you are dead so that your assets are distributed as you wish. Some states allow you to consolidate your health care directive or living will and durable power of

Having these three documents in place ensures your wishes are carried out while you are alive, should you become incapacitated, and after you are dead so that your assets are distributed as you wish.

attorney into one form for all your health care instructions. Check with your estate planner about the requirements in your state.

Trust-Based Estate Planning

High-net-worth individuals and individuals who have assets in different states or those with blended families (e.g., children from two marriages) have a more complex situation that requires a more sophisticated estate plan. They often need to take a trust-based approach to estate planning. Essentially, the trust allows a third party to hold assets on behalf of your beneficiaries. In this plan, you will need a pour-over will, a revocable living trust, health care directive, and a durable power of attorney.

POUR-OVER WILL

If you have a trust in place, your will is only used as a safety net to catch any assets that you didn't transfer into your trust prior to death. In this case, your will is called a pour-over will, and it contains minimal instructions since your revocable living trust is the main document governing your estate plan.

A REVOCABLE LIVING TRUST

Also known as a living trust, a revocable living trust is a legal entity created to hold ownership of an individual's assets. It's generally drawn up by your estate planning attorney.

Once the trust is created, you must sign and date it to execute it. From that point on, you as the person who formed the trust is known as the "grantor." Some grantors prefer their attorney to act as trustee, but in most cases, the grantor also serves as the trustee and continues to control and manage the assets that are placed in the trust. For example, if Mr. Silver formed a trust and transferred assets into it—such as real property, stocks and bonds, or his savings account—he will continue to control and manage the account until his death or incapacity. There is also the option to assign a successor trustee in case the grantor/trustee cannot function or manage because of mental incapacity.

A revocable living trust contains a detailed set of instructions covering three important periods of your life: what happens while you are alive and well, what happens if you become mentally or physically incapacitated, and what happens after your death.

During the first stage, the trust's instructions are simply business as usual. However, it's critical to give some thought about how you want your investments, your bills, and your day-to-day financial responsibilities to be taken care of during the second and third stage and provide this information in your revocable living trust document.

Make sure that aside from your personal information, you name possible beneficiaries (spouse, children, non–family members, or organizations), the name of the trustee who is responsible for managing the trust, how you want the trust assets to be distributed, a list of your assets and their value, a list of tangible assets and how they should be distributed. These include items such as vehicles, jewelry, or household items that have a special meaning. The trust allows you organize and determine to whom you want to give these assets.

As with jointly held bank accounts, payable-on-death accounts, IRA and 401(k) accounts and life insurance policies that require you to fill out a beneficiary designation when you sign up, the assets inside your revocable trust are not subject to probate. They can be distributed immediately to beneficiaries or be managed by the successor trustee to distribute to them over time, depending on how you wrote your trust provisions. By avoiding probate these assets and their beneficiaries remain private—since probate is entered into the public record—and are more efficient and therefore cheaper in terms of attorney fees after your death. Generally, probates also take much longer to complete than the administration of revocable trusts.

WILLS VERSUS TRUSTS

Whether you should take a will-based approach to estate planning or a trust-based approach to your estate plan depends on the complexity of your wealth and your needs in terms of beneficiaries. One advantage a will-based plan has over the trust-based plan is the initial cost. The latter will cost a couple of thousand more than the former in legal fees at the beginning, but if your situation is complex, it's probably worth the investment, as you may save a lot more in attorney fees and taxes after your death.

The main benefits of using a revocable trust include avoiding probate. Probate is very cumbersome and time consuming, which means a major benefit of using a trust-based plan is the hassle and time it saves your beneficiaries as well as affording privacy to your heirs because your estate does not go through probate court and therefore does not become public knowledge. This often becomes more important as people become wealthier. This may also be important for clients with complicated family relationships (such as blended families), as probate provides an easy venue for the challenge of wills and distributions of assets.

A second advantage of the trust is that it allows you to decide whether you want to grant your assets as a lump sum to one beneficiary or control it in more specific detail. For example, after you pass away, then the successor trustee will follow your instruction to manage your money, and this can include, for example, allowing or prohibiting your child to pay $100,000 for a car when he or she turns eighteen. You can make a lot of provisions that you think are reasonable after your death. The trust also gives you the option to control the timing of the distribution. For example, if Mr. Silver leaves $5 million to a very young daughter, she could be affected by having so much money early in life. She could make mistakes. A bad marriage or bad business decision could cost a lot of money. However, with a trust-based plan, you can instruct that distributions be made at different ages, for example, 20 percent at thirty, and then 30 percent at forty-five, and so on. The trust can also be designed so that it's protected from your beneficiaries' creditors. This level of control afforded by the revocable living trust is often called "control from the grave."

TAX CONSIDERATIONS

Despite its advantages and ability to avoid probate, a revocable living trust will not allow you to avoid paying estate taxes. In 2019, federal estate and gift tax exemption is currently $11.4 million per person or $22.8 million for married couples. State taxes vary from state to state. The state estate tax exemption in Minnesota is $2.7 million for 2019. If your estate is over $11.4 million estate tax exemption, a federal estate tax return (Form 709) must be filed to calculate estate taxes due nine months after death. For Minnesotans, if you don't have to pay federal estate taxes, but if your gross estate is over $2.7 million, your estate will have to file an estate tax return in Minnesota to determine tax liability. In addition, income tax returns must be filed on Form 1040 and in your state as usual, just like owning assets in your individual accounts as you use your Social Security number instead of a tax ID for a revocable living trust.

If you have set up a revocable living trust, you can design a credit shelter trust within it so that, upon your death, assets up to the state estate tax exemption amount ($2.7 million) can be transferred to your credit shelter trust. The remainder of your estate can be left directly to your spouse or to a marital trust that benefits him or her. The funds in the credit shelter trust can be used to support your spouse during his or her lifetime. Upon your spouse's death, the balance can go to your children without being included in your spouse's estate (see credit shelter trust diagram on next page). In this instance, the $2.7 million and future growth can be left to the children estate-tax-free. This common strategy is still relevant for married people who live in a state that has estate taxes and exemption amounts that are much lower than federal exemption amounts. If you don't design a credit shelter trust, then all your assets ($2.7 million and more) will go to your spouse, who has over $2.7 million in her name already. If she dies in the same year, she only has one exemption ($2.7 million) to use, therefore causing more assets to be subject to state estate taxes. The estate tax rate in Minnesota ranges from 12 percent to 16 percent; that means there could be over $324,000 estate taxes due in Minnesota.

Regarding life insurance, one way to reduce estate taxes is to set up an irrevocable life insurance trust (ILIT) to be the owner and beneficiary of your policy. You should not plan to withdraw money from this ILIT and must name a trustee to handle the payment of insurance premium. By taking advantage of the annual gifting exemption of $15,000, you can put at least $15,000 a year into your ILIT to pay your annual life insurance premium. If you have a $2 million death benefit (with you as the insured), that benefit will be paid on your death to your ILIT, rather than being counted as part of your estate. Your ILIT assets can be managed to grow and provide income to support your beneficiaries, and the remainder can be distributed to other beneficiaries, such as grandchildren, based on what you wrote in the trust provisions.

An ILIT is different from a revocable living trust because your gift to the ILIT is a complete gift, and you do not access the assets inside the ILIT for your own benefit. Therefore, if you follow the IRS rules properly, the assets including death benefits can bypass your estate to save estate taxes.

Credit Shelter Trust for a Married Couple in Minnesota (Year 2019)

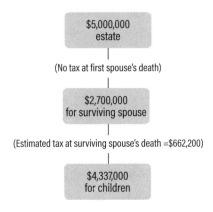

SPOUSE LEAVES EVERYTHING TO SURVIVING SPOUSE

$5,000,000 estate

(No tax at first spouse's death)

$2,700,000 for surviving spouse

(Estimated tax at surviving spouse's death =$662,200)

$4,337,000 for children

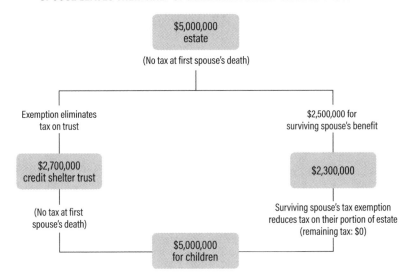

SPOUSE LEAVES THEIR HALF OF ESTATE IN A CREDIT SHELTER TRUST

$5,000,000 estate

(No tax at first spouse's death)

Exemption eliminates tax on trust

$2,500,000 for surviving spouse's benefit

$2,700,000 credit shelter trust

$2,300,000

(No tax at first spouse's death)

Surviving spouse's tax exemption reduces tax on their portion of estate (remaining tax: $0)

$5,000,000 for children

Source: Chan, PLLC Law Offices, www.chanpllc.com.

In 2003, when the estate tax exemption was only $1 million, financial planners had to do a lot of tax planning. It was $5.49 million in 2018. Because the Tax Cuts and Job Act (TCJA) was passed in December 2017, today, with the exemption at $11.4 million ($22.8 for a married couple), fewer people need to do estate tax planning because they won't cross the threshold. However, the exemption is subject to change, and tax planning could one day again become a factor should the exemption come back down.

Seven Estate Planning Mistakes People Make

MISTAKE 1: HAVING NO ESTATE PLAN AT ALL

No one can escape death, yet the biggest mistake people make is not having an estate plan at all, not even a simple will or power of attorney. Thoughtful planning for what may occur after your death is one of the most important things you can do to ensure your personal and financial affairs are handled properly when the inevitable occurs.

> *Thoughtful planning for what may occur after your death is one of the most important things you can do to ensure your personal and financial affairs are handled properly when the inevitable occurs.*

MISTAKE 2. FAILURE TO IMPLEMENT AN ESTATE PLAN PROPERLY

When you sign the legal documents at your attorney's office and are handed a binder with all the documents, you still have more work to do to implement this plan, either doing it yourself or working with your planner and/or attorney. Remember that the beneficiary designation forms for retirement accounts and life insurance policies trump your will. If you have one beneficiary on your retirement account and another on your will, the former will inherit the account. Many people make the mistake of updating their wills to change beneficiaries without changing the beneficiaries for their 401(k) account. This often happens after a divorce.

MISTAKE 3. NOT UPDATING YOUR ESTATE PLAN

Common events that affect your estate plan include changes in family circumstances (such as a child, marriage, or divorce), a new property acquisition, health issues, major tax law changes; and business profits. When you have minor children, you need to make provisions that won't be necessary when they become adults. Your financial situation may change. You may accumulate wealth outside a retirement plan, buy real estate, or set up another profitable business. With each of these life-changing events, it's advisable to consult your estate attorney about more sophisticated estate strategies to transfer your business either to your next generation or key employees.

MISTAKE 4. FAILING TO MAKE GIFTS TO REDUCE THE ESTATE TAX LIABILITY

According to the Internal Revenue code, gifts up to $15,000 a year per donee do not need to be reported. If you have a large estate that may be subject to estate tax if you die, you can start gifting now without using any of your own estate tax exemption. For example, you can give $15,000 to each of your beneficiaries every year while you're alive. If your child has a spouse and four children, you can give them each $15,000, for a total of $90,000 a year tax-free.[31] This allows you to gift a lot of money over the years without having to use up any of your $11.4 million federal exemption or your state exemption.

31 Spouses are exempt from inheritance tax.

MISTAKE 5. CHOOSING THE WRONG PERSON TO HANDLE YOUR ESTATE

Your spouse or child may not be the best person to handle your estate. It's possible that someone else less personally invested can objectively handle the extensive duties and demands required of an executor, trustee, or guardian. You can select a trust company to distribute assets to your beneficiaries rather than making your oldest child a trustee, which could mean the other children would have to ask for money from the trust for many years.

MISTAKE 6. FAILING TO TRANSFER LIFE INSURANCE POLICIES TO AN IRREVOCABLE LIFE INSURANCE TRUST (ILIT)

If, for example, you have a $3 million life insurance policy, that amount will be added to your estate along with your other assets when you die. Although the estate tax exemption is currently high, at $11.4 million, people with very high net worth and a large policy could find themselves over the exemption amount. However, with an ILIT, you can gift at least $15,000 per year to the ILIT to pay annual insurance premiums (reducing your estate), and the death benefit from the insurance policy is paid to this trust upon your death. The trustee then manages and distributes to your beneficiaries. Unlike a revocable living trust, an ILIT avoids estate taxes as long as it follows the IRS rules.

MISTAKE 7. FAILING TO INVESTIGATE TAX LOOPHOLES

If you want to leave stocks to your son during your lifetime, the best strategy is to do this when he is in a low tax bracket and not a dependent on your tax returns. If you transfer $15,000 of stock you have owned for at least a year, with cost basis of $5,000 to him when he is making less than $41,574 income a year, and he sells the stock to realize long-term capital gains of $10,000, he'll end up not owing any capital gains tax because current income tax laws offer no capital gains tax for low income people (i.e., single filer, taxable income of $39,375 in 2019). If you sell the stock and give your son cash, you have to pay either 15 percent or 20 percent long-term capital gain taxes, plus a potential 3.8 percent net investment income tax, as you are not in a low tax bracket. In addition, you don't need to file a gift tax return because the gift is $15,000, the exact annual gift exclusion. Therefore, transferring stock to your son when he is earning very little is a good strategy for keeping more money in your family.

In addition, wealthy business owners with private companies can reduce taxes by forming family limited partnerships to hold the businesses and then gift an ownership interest to children over time. The value of the gift is discounted because the IRS allows minority discounts and lack of liquidity discounts on privately held companies. Minority discount is an economic concept reflecting the notion that a partial ownership interest may be worth less than its proportional share of the total business because a minority position strictly limits investors' ability to make crucial business decisions. A lack-of-liquidity discount means that the value of an interest in a privately held company is less than a publicly traded company because selling an interest in a privately held company is a more costly, uncertain, and time-consuming process than liquidating a position in a publicly traded entity. Therefore, the value of the gift can be discounted when reporting the gifts on gift returns (Form 709).

For example, if your private company is worth $100 million, and you don't transfer any of that to children, they will face a large tax bill when they inherit. However, if over the next twenty years, you give a few shares to each child each year, you can get a 30 percent to 45 percent discount on the gift if your children do not have controlling interests. Over time, therefore, you could pass on a sizeable estate with this strategy. By using this strategy, you are "superleveraging" the value of the company and thus using significantly less estate tax exemption than would otherwise be required.

There are many ways to reduce the legal fees involved in settling your estate by setting up trusts and by properly designating beneficiaries to your life insurance and retirement accounts and turning your individual investments accounts into revocable living accounts. There are also many ways to reduce the tax bill that would be due upon your death during your life. Make sure you talk to your financial planner and your estate attorney to take advantage of all the applicable tax loopholes in place before it's too late.

How to Start a Conversation about Estate Plans

Many people leave estate planning to the last minute. They consider it too private or morbid to discuss. Some people are superstitious, in that they believe talking about something bad will cause it to happen. Talking about estate planning might not be pleasant, but it can help avoid surprises, lead to better financial planning, and promote family harmony.

To make approaching the subject easier, choose your moment. Bring it up when you and your spouse or children are doing something comfortable, such as taking a walk. Alternatively, you can use stories as openers, such as the neighbor who died without a will and caused the family a lot of hardship. Children can tell parents, "I've just updated my own estate plan; is this a good time for you to review yours?"

Depending on your family circumstances and dynamic, it might be better to have a series of small talks than one big one, or it may be better to talk to each individual separately rather than the whole family together. Remember, you know your spouse and his or her communication style, so communicate as a couple. Explain your reasons simply and clearly, and let your adult children know the principles that have guided your decisions.

Taking the time to handle this subject sensitively now will save everyone a headache later.

Final Thoughts

This chapter described a fairly basic approach to the two types of estate plans and some options for reducing taxes, but there are more advanced strategies your wealth manager and estate attorney can advise you on if you have a significant amount of wealth. Make sure you consider some key points when thinking about your own estate plan.

1. Have you reviewed your will in the past five years? If not, it's time to review it to make sure your provisions still meet your objectives. Don't forget to review your durable power of attorney and your health care directive.

2. If your son or daughter has turned eighteen, have they made their own durable power of attorney and healthcare directive? This is very important due to the Health Insurance Portability and Accountability Act (HIPAA) of 1996, which provides data privacy and security provisions for safeguarding medical information. The durable power of attorney and health care directive become even more important when your child is in another state. You may be paying the medical bill, but you will not be allowed to make decisions for your child, and you will not be privy to medical information if you are not their health care agent. Therefore, ask your children to complete these forms.

3. Have you assessed your grown children's financial needs? Your children may be in different financial situations. One may be considerably wealthier than another. Have you considered not dividing your estate equally?

4. Have you considered how to control how your estate is being managed after your death? If one beneficiary is irresponsible and can't be trusted with a $1 million lump sum inheritance, have you examined the different vehicles available that allow you control how the money being managed and distributed to the person in smaller amounts over a longer time frame?

5. Another issue that is growing in importance today but often overlooked is digital assets. Have you discussed with your personal representative where you store your digital assets, such as social media accounts, email passwords, online bill accounts, music, and pictures in the cloud, and provided instructions on how to access them? This is an area to which estate attorneys are starting to pay more attention. You'll need to name someone as the authority to control how they can be accessed after you are gone. If you have a popular website or other online content that has value, it could be lost if you don't properly document these assets.

Estate planning can be a complicated process, so make sure you include an estate attorney and financial planner on your dream team and make sure they are working in tandem to help grow your wealth and guiding you to avoid many of the common mistakes people make when it comes to estate planning. You should also make sure that you consider factors that could derail your retirement and estate planning, such as the need for long-term care. We'll look at this in the next chapter.

CHAPTER 10

Long-Term Care

When her fifty-year old husband suffered a fatal stroke, Lily came to me to figure out what financial decisions she needed to make for her and her daughter in case she ever needed long-term care. Neither she nor her husband had a long-term-care policy because they assumed then wouldn't need it until they were in their seventies or eighties. Like most people their age, they thought they had until their mid- to late fifties to think about it.

Another reason people don't think about long-term care is the same reason they often don't want to think about estate planning—they don't want to dwell on their own disability. No one wants to think about being incapacitated and not being about to perform the six activities of daily living: eating, dressing, bathing, toileting, transferring, and continence.

Unfortunately, the reality is that many of us may have to face this situation at some point in our lives. According to the US Department of Health and Human Services, National Clearinghouse for

No one wants to think about being incapacitated and not being about to perform the six activities of daily living: eating, dressing, bathing, toileting, transferring, and continence.

Long-Term Care Information,[32] approximately 70 percent of those over age sixty-five will require at least some type of long-term-care services during their lifetime, usually for three years and sometimes longer. However, too many people make the mistake of waiting too long to take out a policy to protect them from this eventuality.

Why Plan Early?

More than a decade ago, Congress passed a law to encourage more people, especially baby boomers, to plan early by buying long-term-care insurance. Special tax benefits were offered to motivate people to plan ahead so that they didn't end up on government assistance, either Medicare or Medicaid. I'll talk more about these government programs later in this chapter.

The government's attempt to incentivize individuals to plan early was a good idea for a number of reasons. First, monthly premiums are based upon your age when you apply. This makes premiums less expensive when you're younger. Second, people often wait until their late fifties or later to buy long-term-care insurance, without realizing that predicting the withdrawal of the benefits is problematic—we rarely know when we will need long-term care. A stroke or a heart attack can happen to people in their forties or fifties. Third, coverage

---

32 LongTermCare.gov, "How much care will you need?" (n.d.). Available at https://long-termcare.acl.gov/the-basics/how-much-care-will-you-need.html.

is dependent upon your current health status. If you have a sudden heart attack or injury and have an extended hospital stay, the chances of getting a long-term-care policy afterward dwindles away to almost nothing because of your preexisting condition. It's best to buy your policy when you're young and healthy because not everyone can qualify if they wait longer. This is particularly true for those with a family history of Alzheimer's. These individuals are more likely to use long-term care and for a longer period of time, which makes it even more important to consider buying long-term-care insurance early before you may show any symptoms and buy a longer benefit period than the average of three years.

I bought my policy before I turned forty. No one in my office at the time had ever heard of someone buying a policy this young. I had a good reason. For years, I had been calling home to my mother in China, and every time we spoke, she told me how difficult it had been for her to visit my uncle, who had Alzheimer's and no longer recognized her. He was the oldest brother who put her through college after my grandfather died; he was like a father to her. After nine difficult years with Alzheimer's, my uncle passed away, and this made me realize how important it is to have long-term-care insurance, not just so that you get adequate care as you decline mentally or physically, but also so that the estate you've worked so long to build isn't used to pay for this care or for modifications to your home if, for example, you can't climb the stairs. With the high cost of this care, paying out of pocket could leave your family penniless.

The costs of long-term care often exceed what the average person can pay from their income and other assets. If you think about all the possible health scenarios you could face in your life, it becomes apparent that a financial plan that doesn't include long-term-care planning is not comprehensive. Too often people focus on invest-

Too often people focus on investment planning or college or retirement planning without considering what would happen to their wealth if they were suddenly faced with the cost of long-term care, which can be upward of $7,000 a month.

ment planning or college or retirement planning without considering what would happen to their wealth if they were suddenly faced with the cost of long-term care, which can be upward of $7,000 a month. If you or your spouse needed two or three years of long-term care, that could significantly derail your retirement plans. It's important to be smart about your resources now so that you don't leave yourself open to that amount of risk.

However, very often people do not plan ahead. This is due to a reluctance to think about getting older, developing a disability, becoming less independent, or needing help with personal care. At the same time, they often believe that health insurance, Medicare, and/or disability coverage will cover most long-term-care services should they be needed, so they don't need to dwell on illness and aging. However, health insurance, Medicare, and/or disability coverage is very limited in its coverage, which we will look at in more detail later. That means people are often living with a false sense of comfort that their needs, should they have any, will be taken care of in the long term.

Types of Long-Term Care

Although it's difficult to predict how much or what type of care any one person might need, on average, someone age sixty-five today will need some form of long-term care for three years or more. This care will generally take the form of one of four services:

1. Care or assistance with activities of daily living at home from an unpaid caregiver who can be a family member or friend.

2. Services at home from a nurse, home health/home care aide, therapist, or homemaker.

3. Care in the community.

4. Care in a long-term facility.

While some people need long-term care in a facility for a relatively short period of time while they are recovering from a sudden illness or injury, someone who is disabled from a severe stroke, for example, may need long-term care services on an ongoing basis. It may be possible to receive enough support from a friend or family member, but this person will be unpaid, unless you have enough resources or a long-term-care insurance policy, which I'll discuss later in this chapter.

Some people may need a nurse or home health care aide, and others may be able to receive enough support with the addition of services offered by local community centers, such as adult day care centers and respite centers, as well as benefits coverage advice and tip sheets for taking care of yourself at home. The Administration on Aging's Eldercare[33] is a good source of local information. It also offers statistics to help you with financial planning, such as reviewing your current insurance coverage and your Medicare or Medicare supplement.

If a person's needs can no longer be met at home, moving into a nursing home or other type of facility-based setting for care that

---

33 For information, see http://www.eldercare.gov.

is more extensive for supervision may be the only option. This is often the case with dementia or Alzheimer's. Usually, the condition becomes too difficult for family members to manage, and the patient often ends up requiring long-term supervised care in special facilities.

The Cost of Care

The cost of long-term care in the United States is substantial. The 2018 Genworth[34] long-term-care costs study calculated the average monthly cost of a semiprivate room in a nursing home In Minneapolis at about $8,491.

Unless you have a long-term-care insurance policy, you'll find that existing medical coverage, Medicare, Medicare supplement, or an HMO will provide little if any coverage for long-term-care costs, and most of the services you need will not be covered.

Many people are not aware that Medicare and/or disability coverage do not pay for most long-term-care services. Everyone is entitled to Medicare when they turn sixty-five if they have paid into Medicare / Social Security throughout their life. However, even with a Medicare supplemental plan, most of your long-term-care services will not be covered. Medicare covers long-term-care expenses only if you require skilled medical services—that is, hospitalization—but it will only cover recuperative care for a short period of time. The six activities of daily living are the most common areas where people need help, yet these are not covered by Medicare. You will not receive any help with basic functions you take for granted today, such as getting out of bed and going to the bathroom. Additionally, custodial services, such as nursing care facilities, are not covered beyond one

---

34 Genworth, "Cost of care survey 2018" (n.d.). Available at https://www.genworth.com/aging-and-you/finances/cost-of-care.html.

hundred days, and longer-term home health coverage provided under Medicare Part B is limited to part-time skilled care. It's important to remember that most US nursing homes offer services generally limited to custodial care—assistance with regular activities of daily living—rather than the skilled care found in hospitals, where you are under the supervision of a doctor and tended to by nurses.

Medicaid covers the medical costs of low-income families and individuals. It's the major source of financing for long-term care for the elderly and persons with disabilities, accounting for 42 percent of national spending on long-term care and almost 50 percent of spending on nursing home care. Medicaid provides critical assistance to people with long-term-care needs in the community and nursing homes, covering services often excluded from Medicare and private insurance. Unfortunately, to qualify for Medicaid, you need to have very limited financial resources. For Medicaid to take effect, your portfolio would have to have dwindled to almost nothing. If you are in this situation, you will likely be one of the 62 percent of nursing home residents[35] who rely on Medicaid to pay their long-term-care costs.

If you don't qualify for Medicaid and don't have much in the way of financial resources but own your home, another option for covering long-term-care costs is the reverse mortgage. The reverse mortgage allow you use the equity in your home to pay for services. Review this private financing option carefully to understand all the details, eligibility requirements, and costs.

Most people who have worked with a financial planner during their lives and followed a careful financial plan of a balanced investment portfolio, retirement accounts, life insurance, and the other products we've talked about in this book will find themselves too

---

35 Henry J. Kaiser Family Foundation, "Medicaid's role in nursing home care" (June 20, 2017). Available at http://www.kff.org/Medicaid/2186.cfm.

Look at your assets. If you need care for five years, do you have these resources? If you use your portfolio to cover these costs, what will that mean for your spouse's standard of living now and in retirement?

wealthy to qualify for Medicaid. This means that without long-term care insurance, you could end up exhausting your stock portfolio to pay for your care. Look at your assets. If you need care for five years, do you have these resources? If you use your portfolio to cover these costs, what will that mean for your spouse's standard of living now and in retirement?

Ultimately, I have found that the best option to plan ahead for long-term care is to buy long-term-care insurance, especially if you are still relatively healthy and not too old. You can work with your financial planner to run scenarios using a tool like the Echo Dashboard to show the potential costs of long-term care and see how this will impact your financial plan. Comparing the scenario of not buying the insurance versus buying the insurance by choosing the age (i.e., seventy-five or eighty) that you think you are more likely to incur long-term-care expenses will help you see the difference in your projected portfolio value at the end of your life.

Once this insurance policy is in place, you are eligible to collect benefits when you are unable to perform two or more daily living activities, or if you become cognitively impaired, such as having Alzheimer's or dementia.

If you do buy a long-term-care policy, make sure you review it to understand how long-term-care insurance works before your long-term-care costs arise.

How Long-Term-Care Insurance Works

Nursing homes emerged in the 1960s to provide long-term care outside the family. At the time, many people had no option but to sell their homes or deplete their savings to pay for this care. This gave rise to a need for an insurance plan to cover these costs. By the late 1970s, long-term-care insurance was being offered across the country. Unfortunately, by the 2000s, it became clear that insurance providers had underestimated the rise in health care costs and the number of people who would need care and claim benefits. Many could not make a profit in this product line and decided not to offer long-term-care insurance products anymore. Today, there are only a few insurance companies that offer long-term-care insurance. Congress revised the tax laws to allow insurance companies to design life insurance policies and add broader long-term-care benefit riders. Today, therefore, there are two types of policies: a traditional long-term-care insurance policy and a hybrid long-term-care policy (life insurance with long-term-care benefits).

Traditional Long-Term-Care Policy

There are two types of traditional long-term-care policies: reimbursement and indemnity. When you buy a traditional reimbursement policy, for example, a monthly benefit of $5,000 for five years, for a total benefit of $300,000, the insurance company reimburses your long-term-care expenses up to the benefit amount per month. If your expenses are $7,000 a month, the policy will still only reimburse you to the benefit maximum of $5,000 a month. With this policy, you can choose an inflation rider to receive a higher benefit amount. If you're younger than sixty-five, it's important to have an insurance rider so that your benefits keep step with inflation—$5,000 today won't buy you the same services ten or twenty years from now.

While the reimbursement type of long-term-care policies are cheaper, offer more variety, and are more readily available than an indemnity policy, the drawback is that you must incur qualified long-term-care expenses in order to get reimbursed. The indemnity policy pays cash, and you can decide how to spend it, such as hiring your daughter to take care of you at home. Generally, indemnity policies are at least 30 percent more expensive than reimbursement policies; therefore, you must compare and decide if getting paid in cash up to the benefit amount when you cannot perform two or more daily living activities is very important to you.

The major drawback of both traditional reimbursement and indemnity polices is that future premiums are uncertain. As has happened in the past, after a decade or so, an insurance company may realize it hasn't priced its product correctly. It then applies to the state to increase premiums. If you were paying a $2,000 annual premium, you could find yourself paying more during your lifetime. This increase is not based on your individual health condition; it's applied to everybody in the same risk class. Your only option to keep the policy is to choose to pay more to keep the same benefits or pay less to reduce the current benefits.

Hybrid Long-Term-Care Policy

On August 17, 2006, President George W. Bush signed into law the Pension Protection Act of 2006, which contains a section that made federal law, particularly individual tax law, more hospitable to hybrid products involving long-term-care insurance and annuities and life insurance. Tax-free exchanges are possible between annuities and life insurance. This means that money in an annuity can be moved into life insurance without paying taxes, but taking money out of an annuity (by means other than the prescribed annuity payout) for other purposes generally results in the need to pay taxes on at least a portion of the money taken out. The Pension Protection Act expanded the scope of tax-free transfers called "1035 Exchange" to also include exchanges of life insurance and annuity contracts for the new hybrid life insurance contracts with long-term-care benefits (with some exceptions).

The hybrid long-term-care insurance policies have gained popularity because insurance companies designed life insurance products with long-term-care benefits and the insured can make a 1035 exchange to use the cash value of a life insurance policy to pay for this new hybrid life insurance with long-term-care benefits without paying taxes on the gains inside the current policy. This hybrid product offers death benefits and long-term-care benefits that are both income-tax-free. I like to use whole life with long-term-care benefits, as the death benefit's designed to be small to reduce cost. Not all hybrid products are created equal. Some offer no elimination period at home; some offer a return of premium feature.

The most attractive feature for the hybrid product is that the premium cost is fixed, and the insurance company cannot increase premiums after the contract is issued. Some products have a one-time pay feature that ranges from $60,000 to $100,000 in premiums, and some offer payments over seven or ten years to make this easier for middle income and younger people. It's attractive to people who have a large enough investment portfolio that they can afford to allocate 5 to 10 percent of their investment portfolio to buy this type of policy.

There are a number of advantages to the hybrid policy. Some hybrid products offer reimbursement or indemnity (but at a lower benefit amount). First, it pays the benefit in cash if you choose the indemnity feature at the time of claim, which means you can pay it to anyone who is providing care, even if that's a family member. Second, it gives you the ability to lock in your premium because the premium is often paid in one payment. Third, it allows you leave a tax-free death benefit to your beneficiary if you die before needing any long-term care. Fourth, you have the option to access the asset in this policy if you decide someday that you don't need long-term-care coverage; some products can be surrendered without charge in the first year and others offer a full return of your premium benefit in year fifteen.

When working with Lily to devise her long-term-care strategy after her husband died, she expressed two concerns. She had $2 million in her portfolio that she wanted to protect and leave to her daughter, and she didn't want to have to worry about how to find the best care should she need long-term care and didn't want this burden to fall to her daughter.

Because Lily had significant assets, we were able to structure a hybrid policy to minimize her life insurance costs. She could afford to pay the hybrid policy's single-pay premium of $104,000 for a policy that came with a death benefit of $120,000 and a total long-term-care benefit of $405,000. It included a ninety-day elimination period for a nursing home facility, assisted living facility, and facility hospice care, but no elimination period for home health care, care coordination, home modification, caregiving training, and adult day care center.

This policy structure translated into a long-term-care payout of $6,000 monthly for six years. It had a 5 percent simple inflation rider so that the benefits would grow to $855,000 by age eighty. If she started using long-term-care benefits at age eighty, the monthly benefit would be $11,250. This addressed her first concern.

To address her second concern, Lily's policy also included coordination of benefits—that is, the insurance company would coordinate with different parties to deliver the long-term-care services. With one phone call, they could send local long-term-care specialists to her home to assess the situation and devise a plan of care with her and her daughter that included staying at home if preferred or, if not, recommending and moving her to different types of facilities.

By investing $104,000 in her policy one payment at the age of fifty-five, the internal rate of return (IRR) on her long-term-care benefits at age eighty worked out to be 7.82 percent[36] per year, tax-free. This is the tax-free return if she starts collecting long-term-care benefits at age eighty and uses 100 percent of the benefits in this contract. If she needs care earlier than age eighty, then the IRR would be even higher. This is a good rate of return on any investment. It also gave her the security of knowing that she would have a $6,000 a month benefit for six years, adjusted for inflation, whenever she needed long-term care. When she died, her daughter would get a $120,000 tax-free death benefit if she hadn't used the long-term-care benefits.

For Lily, this approach to her planning gave her peace of mind. She used 5 percent of her portfolio for a one-time purchase of her policy and allowed me to manage the other 95 percent of her wealth. She then had a balanced investment portfolio in place as well as an insurance policy backed by a big life insurance company that had been in business for 151 years that would protect her wealth should she need long-term care. It also offered her independence on her own terms. She would not be forced to go somewhere she didn't want to

36 This is internal rate of return (IRR) guaranteed by this insurance company based on the insurance contract. Financial planner cannot guarantee a rate of return.

go, and she had the flexibility to receive the best care possible and still have that tax benefit.

Lily's wishes are shared by most people, and the key to manifesting them is to plan ahead to ensure greater independence should you need care. Most people want to stay at home rather than go into a nursing home; however, without planning there is a strong possibility that you won't receive the services you want; will have to rely on government assistance, where your choices will be limited to what the government provides in its facilities; or will end up depleting your wealth to pay for what you do want.

You have worked throughout your life to build wealth. With careful planning and the right insurance, you will be able to maintain your dignity and standard of living, and preserve your estate for your heirs at the end of life.

Final Thoughts

Too often, people work on their investment portfolio, college funds, their retirement plan, and estate plan, but don't plan for long-term care, only to find the substantial costs of this care exhausts their wealth and undermines a lifetime's work.

Don't leave it until too late to start planning for your health and long-term-care needs. You never know when you will need care. Think about others you are obligated to support, such as your parents. If you are your parents' representative, review their estate plan as well as your own. Have your financial planner meet with their estate planning attorney to review their financial plan, and consider adding some long-term-care planning. If you find a gap, an early-and-often review may give you time to adjust. If they don't have money for a long-term-care policy or don't qualify, this gives you time to strategize a way to cover costs should the need arise. Very often, people reach age fifty and think their parents haven't done enough, and it's too late to help them. This isn't necessarily true. Talk to your financial planner and insurance agent about available options.

It's also important to make sure your children know that you have done this planning for yourself. A common worry children have is, "Oh my goodness, if my parents are not prepared for long-term care, I will have to somehow plan for paying for it." This means that one of the best gifts you could give to your children to free them from worry is letting them know that you have done some planning for proper care for your later years. Talk to them about your long-term-care plan, and inform them where you would like to receive care.

When it comes to long-term planning, ask yourself the following questions:

1. Are you doing your regular checks on your financial plan, estate plan, wills, and trusts with your financial planner, and have you discussed a plan to pay for potential long-term-care costs?

2. How would you pay for long-term-care costs of $6,000 to $8,000 per month for three years if you need the care starting next month?

3. How do you feel about using possibly 5–10 percent of your portfolio to invest in a long-term-care policy that would provide the most flexibility in how you want to receive the best care?

4. Have you discussed your plan with your children or grandchildren so that they don't have to worry?

Talk to your life and health insurance agent. In some states, he or she can take extra training to also sell long-term-care insurance in addition to life insurance. Buying long-term-care insurance is one of the best ways to protect the wealth that you spent your whole life growing and one of the best ways to ensure you have assets to leave your children or a charity of your choice.

We'll look at charitable giving in the next chapter.

CHAPTER 11

Charitable Giving

No book on financial planning would be complete without a chapter of charitable giving. When you've reached a point where your wealth management strategies have paid off, and you are comfortable in life, giving back is something you can do that will bring a great sense of fulfillment to your life and allow you to leave a legacy.

Americans are generous people. Each year, 10.2 percent of the country's GDP is donated to charitable causes, compared to only half that amount by Canadians and socially conscious Europeans.[37] However, there is still a lot of confusion about giving and ways to give. Most people write a check and fail to benefit from the tax reduction opportunities to maximize the good they are going to do for themselves and for their charity of choice.

---

37 Daniel J. Mitchell, "Americans Are More Charitable than 'Socially Conscious' Europeans," *Foundation for Economic Education* (February 3, 2017). Available at https://fee.org/Americans-are-more-charitable-than-socially-conscious-Europeans.

Most people write a check and fail to benefit from the tax reduction opportunities to maximize the good they are going to do for themselves and for their charity of choice.

For example, one of my clients, Ms. Garnet, was reluctant to sign estate documents. She was divorced and had no children, and all of her friends were financially well off and didn't need her money. Quite simply, she didn't know what to do with her estate. I explained that she could do some really good work with her money, and we set about identifying causes she supported, and she could benefit from taking charitable deductions now when her income is high before she retires. For example, setting up a donor-advised fund and putting money or assets in the fund would give her a tax write-off in the present and allow her to pick various charities to benefit later. She could also name her donor-advised fund as the beneficiary of more assets from her estate when she died.

If, like Ms. Garnet, you are already giving, or want to know the right way to give, this chapter will offer you guidance on doing so more effectively, not only to benefit the charity of your choice, but also to give you a sense of satisfaction that can enrich your life.

What Is Charitable Giving?

A charitable donation is a gift made by an individual or an organization to a nonprofit organization, charity, or private foundation. Charitable donations can be made in cash, real estate, motor vehicles, appreciated securities, or other assets or services. It does not include giving gifts to your friends or family. You cannot, for example, donate $1,000 to your dog, but you can donate that money to an animal rescue organization. From a personal financial planning perspective, contributions to a charity can be deducted on your income tax returns if you choose itemized deductions instead of standard deductions. However, in order to take the charitable deduction on the tax return, the gift has to be made—-that is, it cannot come back to you.

People often think that to give charitably and reduce significant taxes, they must set up a private foundation. However, unless you are very rich and can set aside a couple of million dollars right away, a foundation isn't a viable option, due to the setup cost, the ongoing tax reporting, and the personnel needed to manage it. There are far more feasible options available, which we'll look at in this chapter.

Other people think that they don't have enough money to make charitable donations, but there are ways to give as little as $1,500 per year. Creating a small scholarship fund is one option. Additionally, being able to give clothes, household goods, or other valuables should not be discounted. These are all deductible and can be listed on Schedule A of your federal tax return. You can save yourself several hundred dollars in taxes from this simple practice of noncash donations, as long as you keep good records, and you can benefit the recipient in the process.

The rest of this chapter will focus on the five common mistakes most people make when gifting and the nine best practices for giving that will help you reach your gifting goals.

Five Common Giving Mistakes

People often reach a point in their life where careful planning has led them to a place where they can afford to give back and have the desire to do so. Unfortunately, they can oversimplify the process and make the following mistakes that don't maximize the benefit of their gift.

DONATING TAX-INEFFICIENT ASSETS, USING CHECKS, PAYROLL DEDUCTIONS, OR CREDIT CARDS

When you write a check, make payroll deductions, give cash, or charge a donation to your credit card, you are using tax-inefficient assets to give. Many people have stocks in taxable accounts that have appreciated over the years, and donating these are much more effective than the cash options. We'll look at this in more detail later in this chapter.

NOT KEEPING TRACK OF DONATIONS, DISORGANIZATION, OR FRUSTRATION

Failing to track donations causes a lot of stress during tax season. People get bogged down trying to get receipts organized and trying to decide what is tax deductible. This can be remedied by having a system in place to track donations throughout the year. If you donate household items, including clothes, ask for a receipt each time, and take pictures of the items you donate at the charity location. File them in a folder, and write down your estimated thrift shop value on the receipt. You must obtain a written acknowledge from a charity for any single contribution of $250 or more before you can claim a charitable donation on your tax returns.

SELLING APPRECIATED ASSETS WITHOUT TAX PLANNING OR CHARITABLE GIVING PLANNING

Failing to do tax planning before selling appreciated assets, such as land, a business, or appreciated stock, could mean missing opportunities to save taxes while you benefit the charity of your choice. We'll look at this more in the next section.

RUSHING TO MAKE DONATIONS AT THE END OF THE YEAR

People often find themselves needing deductions and rushing to write a check in the last week of the tax year, without accounting for the holiday season. To have a gift acknowledged, a written receipt is needed, but trying to get this issued and mailed out to you from a charity over the holiday season is impractical.

GIVING STOCK IN TOO-SMALL AMOUNTS

A stock transfer strategy won't be of much use to someone who wants to give $500 to ten different organizations each year because of the fees and paperwork involved in so many transactions.

Nine Best Practices for Charitable Giving

There are many practices and strategies available to ensure that you are effective in reaching your giving goals, from setting up special funds, considering alternative beneficiaries on your retirement accounts, and benefiting from charitable contribution deductions while you're alive.

GIFT APPRECIATED SECURITIES TO AVOID CAPITAL GAINS TAX

We have had over a decade of strong stock market returns, which means the capital gain implications from selling investments can be significant for some investors. One way to reduce this tax bill is to donate your appreciated securities, rather than cash or writing a check, to a charity.

If you have held these securities for more than a year, it's also possible to deduct the full, fair market value of the stocks on your tax return. For example, if you bought $10,000 of a stock many years ago that's now worth $80,000, you could sell the stock and recognize

There are many practices and strategies available to ensure that you are effective in reaching your giving goals, from setting up special funds, considering alternative beneficiaries on your retirement accounts, and benefiting from charitable contribution deductions while you're alive.

the long-term gain of $70,000, but you would only walk away with $60,000 because you have to pay federal capital gains tax of 15 percent or 20 percent. Alternatively, you could give the stock to a charity. Because the charity doesn't pay tax, it would receive the full $80,000 benefit, and you receive a potential income deduction on the tax return of up to the $80,000 value. This could save you tens of thousands of dollars in taxes. Added together, the total benefit to you and charity may be close to double what you would receive if you sold the stock. In this scenario, everybody gets to use that full $80,000 to do good, which means everyone wins.

If you have not decided on a charity to support but still want to reduce your tax bill, you can set up a donor-advised fund. Establishing this fund is also a good idea if you have appreciated securities in your taxable accounts.

A donor-advised fund can be best described as a charitable investment account that provides simple, flexible, and efficient ways to manage charitable giving.

Once you put money or assets into a donor-advised fund, it becomes an irrevocable transfer to a public charity with the specific intent of funding charitable gifts. I recommend using the American

Endowment Foundation (AEF)[38] to set up donor-advised funds because it's low cost and offers great support to financial planners and individuals, such as helping them identifying causes and which charities are well managed and doing good work. The AEF is a nonprofit organization already qualified under the IRS code to help people set up donor-advised funds. The financial planner can advise clients on which assets to put into the fund for overall tax efficiency, but the client doesn't need to determine which charity or charities he or she wants to donate to in order to put assets into the account. Neither is the client restricted to one charity, or the same charity each year. For example, if a financial planner advised a client to allocate $30,000 in assets to the fund one year, the client has the option to make a grant request of the AEF to pay $10,000 to three different charities. In addition, the client could for example choose to give $30,000 to the American Cancer Society one year and the ASPCA the next year. You can also choose not to request any grants, allowing the money to grow for future grant requests.

In this way, the AEF serves as the administrator of the fund. The brokerage account itself is set up by your financial planner who can be named as your investment advisor with discretionary trading authorization, but you can determine the grant amounts to the charity or charities of your choice. You can also deduct the full market value of this stock as charitable contributions in the year you donate to your donor-advised fund as long as the stock has been held by you for at least one year.

If you open an account through AEF, your account title would be "American Endowment Foundation FBO Your Fund Name" (e.g., Schwartz Family Charitable Fund). Your financial planner can still manage this account at a brokerage firm such as TD Ameritrade

38 See www.AEFonline.org for more information.

even though you gave the stock to the foundation and technically no longer own this account as long as your planner has an agreement with the foundation and brokerage firm to be able to trade in your account. Having your financial planner manage your fund means you know how it's being managed. You receive regular performance reports. Your financial planner can also decide when to sell the stock. For example, I meet with my clients twice a year to plan ahead. If they normally give twice a year to several charities, I manage the portfolio to ensure there is enough cash there for the grant amount, but I don't decide where the money is donated. How much and to whom to give is up to the clients.

A donor-advised fund is much cheaper to set up and maintain than a private foundation and has fewer restrictions when it comes to income tax deductions, tax on investment income, and annual distribution requirements. AEF has no setup fees, and its annual fees are up to 0.60 percent per year based on the account balance. You can deduct up to 60 percent of adjusted gross income if you donate cash and up to 30 percent if you donate appreciated assets. In addition, unlike private foundation, you don't have to file tax returns for this donor-advised fund because the fund is administered by the AEF, and it files its own annual tax return.

Naming a successor to your donor-advised fund offers a way to engage your children and grandchildren with your charitable values and educate them in the ways they can administer the fund to support charities they care about.

TIME YOUR GIFTS WISELY

It's always a good idea to time your gifts wisely based on your income expectations. If you expect to receive a large bonus or plan to exercise your stock options or sell your business for a profit and know this will put you in the next tax bracket, consider increasing your charitable giving that year to reduce your taxable income.

For example, one of my clients, Ms. Redd, sold her business and was facing a substantial tax bill that year. She had established philanthropic goals and was donating $8,000 a year in cash to her various charities. To help offset the spike in income in that year, we set up a donor-advised fund into which she contributed $200,000, which she then claimed as a charitable deduction. This reduced her tax burden and set aside funds to cover her $8,000 a year charitable giving for the next 25 years.

However, if you have a donor-advised fund already set up, and you have identified the low-cost-basis stocks in your nonretirement account to donate to the fund right before year-end, you can reduce the tax liability on the additional income generated from a nonqualified stock option exercise even near year-end. As with Ms. Redd above, this transfer would cover many years of charitable donations to come. This is another case in which last-minute giving can offset your tax bill if you time your gifts and gift strategies wisely.

NAME A CHARITY AS THE BENEFICIARY OF YOUR RETIREMENT PLAN

After years of prudent financial planning, you may find yourself approaching retirement with enough income-generating assets that you don't need the money from your retirement account because you have pension, Social Security, and nonretirement accounts. If you name your son, for example, as beneficiary to a traditional IRA or 401(k) plan, he will be liable for estate taxes and income taxes when he withdraws from the IRA if your estate is valued above the state estate tax exemption in your state ($2.7 million in Minnesota for example) and also if it's above the current federal estate tax exemption

The benefit of giving to charities during your lifetime is that you are alive to see the positive impact your wealth is having, which can be immensely gratifying.

amount ($11.4 million per individual). In other words, your son could receive less than fifty cents on the dollar from your IRA account, depending on his income tax bracket and your estate tax situation.

However, should you name the charity as the beneficiary of your retirement plan, it will receive 100 percent of funds because it's tax exempt. Therefore, if you plan on leaving money to a charity at your death, consider leaving your traditional IRA or 401(k) plan balances to the charity by having the money paid out from one of your IRAs directly. If your son inherits your nonretirement accounts (preferably from your revocable living trust to avoid probate), the appreciated securities receive a stepped-up basis to the market value on the day of your death; that means he doesn't have to pay much in capital gains taxes if he sells them soon.

If you don't want to leave your entire retirement account to a single charity, or if you only want to leave a certain amount to charity and want to give the rest to friends or family members, you can set up separate IRAs and name a different beneficiary on each account.

DON'T WAIT UNTIL YOU DIE TO MAKE GIFTS

The benefit of giving to charities during your lifetime is that you are alive to see the positive impact your wealth is having, which can be immensely gratifying. What's more, in gifting while you're alive, you can take advantage of income tax deductions and remove more assets from your estate for tax purposes. If you die before year-end, you can instruct your spouse to make these donations by having this discussion in advance, which will also give you an income tax deduction for that year. This allows you to give more money to your heirs or the charity of your choice.

GIFT YOUR IRA ASSETS EVERY YEAR

If you are over 70.5, you should consider gifting your IRA assets every year. At this age, you must withdraw the required minimum distribution (RMD) from your IRA, which the IRS calculates based on your life expectancy. The tax penalty for failing to do so is 50 percent of the amount overdue for withdrawal. If you don't need the money to live on, a good strategy is to gift it to a charity. You can transfer up to $100,000 per year directly to charity, tax-free. You won't get an income tax deduction for the gift, but by gifting it instead of adding it to your gross income, you can avoid increasing your tax burden that year as well as avoiding the heavy penalty for failing to withdraw the RMD from your IRA.

BUNDLE MULTIPLE YEARS' DONATIONS

The Tax Cuts and Jobs Act of 2017 (TCJA) simplified the individual income tax for millions of households. It doubled the standard deduction, which meant millions of people are now better off taking the newly expanded standard deduction, instead of itemizing deductions.

For example, a retired couple over age sixty-five who didn't have mortgage interest found that the state income tax and property tax deductions were capped at $10,000. They normally donated $10,000 a year. Between these two lines, they only had an itemized deduction of $20,000, which is below the standard deduction of $27,000 in 2019. However, if they gifted three years of charitable contributions in one year, they would have $30,000 in charitable deductions along with the $10,000 property tax deduction, to give them a $40,000 itemized deduction in 2019. If they don't want to give more in 2020, they can choose the standard deduction of $27,000 (adjusted for inflation).

If you know which charity you want to support but don't want to set up a donor-advised fund, this is a good alternative strategy for effective charitable giving.

SET UP SCHOLARSHIP FUNDS

If you support education, and you want to help students achieve their higher education goals, another way to gift to charitable causes is to set up your own scholarship at your alma mater by donating cash or securities. You can start gifting a small amount as a scholarship, for example, $1,500, or a larger amount each year. You can also set your own criteria for qualifying for the fund. Universities have scholarship committees to select the winner based on your written criteria. I received multiple small scholarships each year when I was attending Winona State University (WSU), so it was important to me that I reciprocated by setting up a scholarship fund at WSU for one international student enrolled in the College of Business. It has been very rewarding to hear the winners' personal stories and learn how my scholarship has brought them closer to achieving their American dream.

TAKE ADVANTAGE OF LOW INTEREST RATES WITH A CHARITABLE LEAD TRUST

There are two basic types of charitable trusts: charitable remainder trusts (CRTs) and charitable lead trusts (CLTs). Today's relatively low-interest-rate environment affects both.

You can take advantage of today's low interest rates with a CRT, which is a tax-exempt irrevocable trust that is designed to reduce the taxable income of individuals by first dispersing income to the beneficiaries of the trust for a specified period of time and then donating the remainder of the trust to the designated charity. In other words, a CRT provides you and your beneficiary with a stream of income over your lifetime and then turns over what remains of the trust to the charity at the end of the trust term. The tax deduction you can take on your contribution to the CRT depends on the present value of the remainder interest in the trust.

The CLT works the opposite way. It's an irrevocable trust designed to provide financial support to one or more charities for a period of time. With a CLT, the trust makes annual contributions to charity and distributes the remaining asset to family members or other beneficiaries at the end of the trust term. You receive a deduction based on the present value of the amount the CLT distributes to a charity. Any appreciation of the trust beyond the IRS calculated interest rate results in a tax-free gift to your beneficiaries. When rates are low, the opportunity to generate such asset return can be especially strong. In this way, the currently low interest rate environment works in favor of the CLT by increasing its present value and thus increasing your potential tax deduction.

The benefits of the CLT include reducing the tax costs of transferring an asset to your heirs. The amount of the term of the payments to the charity can be determined in advance, which will reduce transfer taxes due on the principal when it reverts to your heirs, and all the stock appreciation in the trust can be given tax-free to those named in your trust.

If you or your financial planner believe putting assets in a trust could be a good strategy for your investment plan, talk to your estate attorney about creating a trust document and your financial planner about funding it with proper investments.

INSPIRE YOUR HEIRS

Another great practice for charitable giving during your lifetime is the ability it gives you to share your passion and the causes you support with your children and grandchildren. Letting them know your values and how you help others will help them continue your good work after you are gone as well as instill in them a responsibility to help those in need.

Aside from your financial legacy, you can leave a moral legacy. You can show your heirs that money is a potent force. If managed well, it can do much good in the world. Not only will this understanding benefit those less fortunate, it will have the added benefit of rewarding your children with the satisfaction that comes from making a positive contribution to society.

Final Thoughts

Once you have achieved financial independence, ask what else your money can do for you. Most people want money to provide security, freedom and, hopefully, joy. One way to maximize the joy of having money is to support the community, people, and causes about which you care. Thankfully, statistics show that many people who have reached a place of means are generously thinking about others and seeking ways to increase their well-being.

As you can see, charitable giving is not as simple as just writing a check. You can make a substantial difference in how your wealth is distributed and in how others benefit from it, if you follow some of the effective strategies we've looked at in this chapter.

When it comes to deciding on a charity and creating a charitable giving plan, here are some questions to ask yourself:

1. How much did you donate to charities last year in cash? Look at the itemized deductions on Schedule A of your federal tax return. If this is a few thousand dollars, you are making a substantial contribution that warrants a review of effective strategies available to you.

2. Do you have at least one security that has appreciated over 30 percent in your nonretirement account? Talk to your financial planner about tax strategies that can benefit you and your charity.

3. Have you decided which charities to support? Who else needs to be involved in this decision? Use resources such as the AEF to help you identify how much and to whom you want to donate.

4. Which past donations have given you the most satisfaction? Why? This will help you craft your plan and your goals moving forward into retirement and beyond.

5. Have you experienced any frustrations in making your donations or keeping track of them? This indicates that it's time to talk to your financial planner and get a plan in place to make your charitable giving more effective and painless.

After a lifetime of hard work and sound financial planning, many people find themselves able to leave a legacy. Part of achieving the American dream for me was being able to give back. As of writing, I expect to have another twenty or so years left in my working life. I have already earned more than enough to retire, but I continue to work because it's my way of helping others with my skills and with my wealth.

Many of my clients could retire now or in five years, but they are asking the question: What does retirement mean to me? There are only so many days you can play golf. They want something more to do. There is a big change in identity here, and many people don't want to be "just a retiree." This is a perfect environment for charitable giving and/or becoming more engaged in their communities, which will also help people who are transitioning from being a busy executive or business owner into retirement.

As you can see, charitable giving strategies are a good solution for your health and well-being and for the well-being of the community. Remember, you don't have to wait until you're wealthy to think about charitable giving. You just need a solid strategy that is tailored to your means. Nor do you have to donate money or assets. You could also donate your time and skills. This allows you to connect with people who are not only good for your career and wealth building but also for your health and well-being. Networking with like-minded people is a great way to explore areas that can make your life more meaningful.

As you finish reading this book and have many strategies to take away to simplify managing your wealth, I hope you will give some thought to giving back too. Remember, this book, like your life, is about more than just investing and make the most money possible. It's also about how to utilize all your resources to maximize your return on life.

CHAPTER 12

Final Thoughts

In the pages of this book, I have offered you a financial planning framework that you can use to find manageable ways to grow your wealth. While not everything in this book will be relevant to every situation you face or indeed to every reader, I recommend that you find two or three takeaways on which to really reflect.

As I have stressed many times throughout this book, the first step in any plan should be goal setting. Goals must be specific and have deadlines. Once done, the next step should be reflecting on which actions you can take to have a meaningful impact. This could be as simple as committing to reading a blog entry once a week on an area relevant to you. It may be making time to see your financial planner to discuss areas that have been overlooked in your financial plan or ask some of the questions posed in this book. This could be adjusting your charitable giving strategy or refining other areas that are working but could work better.

The first step in any plan should be goal setting. Goals must be specific and have deadlines. Once done, the next step should be reflecting on which actions you can take to have a meaningful impact.

Another area worth reflecting on is your possible behavioral biases. Challenge yourself to make sure you are not making wealth management harder than it needs to be. Next, it's advisable to reflect on your dream team and examine how they are performing compared to how you now know they should be performing. If you're not happy with your relationship with team members or their relationship with each other, think about switching them out. The Financial Planning Association[39] has a search function to find planners in your area and based on your criteria. I recommend you interview three and choose the one you trust and who listens to and understands you and your goals.

Another point of action or reflection could be examining your dreams. I hope that women who grew up with the stereotype that boys are better in math and science can see that this isn't true and that this profession offers them a viable opportunity to take control of their own plan, ask the right questions, and evaluate the performance of their own team. Remember, a man is not a plan. Many grown women with real jobs seem to think they can put off financial planning—everything from contributing to a 401(k) plan to buying a house. Too often, women say, "This will all be taken care of when I get married." You should not wait to make major financial decisions until you get married because the reality is that Prince Charming may never come. With 50 percent of marriages ending in divorce,

39 See http://www.plannersearch.org for more information.

saying "I have a husband who manages our investments" is not a solution. Women earn about 75 percent of men's income. Women also live longer and spend more time out of the workplace. Women spend an average of eleven years out of the workforce caring for a relative or children. That time is usually spent not saving for retirement. Women spend as many years caring for their elderly parents as they do raising their children. The fact is, an increasing number of women will end up managing money on their own because they've been divorced or widowed or have never married. All these unique challenges for women make planning for a financial future even more important.

As I mentioned at the outset, one of my goals in writing this book was to show you that it's possible to take control of your finances and financial future by learning enough to work with a team. Even if you aren't good with numbers, it's possible to find someone trustworthy who is.

As Malcolm X said, "Education is the passport to the future, for tomorrow belongs to those who prepare for it today." In addition to reading books and blogs, you can learn from people, experts, and peers. Cultivate a group of people who know you well, including perhaps a spouse/partner, mentor, or trusted friend. These people will point out blind spots in your thinking as you try new ideas for business and personal growth.

As we now come to the end, remember that you don't have to be rich to start planning for your financial future. You can start from wherever you are. Remember, your future is yours, so believe in yourself, believe that success is achievable as long as you are willing to dream, learn from failures, plan meticulously and deliberately, and then take small actions to get you to the next goal. Monitor your plan over time, and position yourself to seize opportunities as they arise.

This doesn't mean living with only the end in mind. Your dreams may change, so be flexible and adaptable, and, above all, remember that wealth management can be complicated, but it doesn't have to be, so get the right help and enjoy the journey.

ACKNOWLEDGMENTS

This is the last part of writing a book, and I've found it hard to begin. So many people have contributed to my writing this book, and so many people have influenced me as a person. I've been blessed with family members, friends, colleagues, teachers, bosses, and clients who have widened my perspective. I'd like to especially thank those who have helped me grow as a person, as a financial planner, and as a writer.

I want to thank my parents (Guobin Huang and Huiying Zhang) who started their lives in very poor villages in southern China and eventually became educators in Shenzhen. You're my first teachers, who instilled me with a love for reading and a respect for education. I appreciate how you raised me and all the extra love you gave me.

I thank my daughter Nina, who is imaginative and understands that I am a career-loving mother. You are my treasure! I don't want you to follow in my footsteps; I want you to take the path next to me and go further than I could have ever dreamed possible.

I am also grateful for having Victor Wong and Hansheng Chen as my two sponsors who made it possible for me to come to the United States to study finance by myself at age twenty. Tony Wong, my mother's cousin in Hong Kong, asked his brother Victor to help me in 1991. Your generosity toward my mother and me has changed many people's lives.

And massive thanks to my uncle Yuanfa Zhang, who not only believed in me but also helped me navigate the American university system. You helped me adjust to my new life in this country during the first critical year. I still remember how you rode your bicycle looking for me in the dark while the snow was falling down in Moscow, Idaho, when I got lost after my last class on my first day at the University of Idaho.

I want to thank the faculty at Winona State University, especially Professor Jim Hurley, Terri Markos of the office of international studies and cultural outreach, and Marie Bush of the budget office. My college life was enriched because of you and other people on campus who paid special attention to educating a new international student. Professor Hurley, the accounting principles I learned from you are still useful today. Terri, the international cross-cultural experiences you facilitated helped me gain global perspective by introducing my own culture to this community. Marie, working with you on managing the university's budget using Excel gave me insight into a nonprofit organization's finances.

Kristine Johnston, my boss at KPMG Personal Financial Planning Group, was kind and patient with me as I explored the new field of tax planning for high net worth corporate executives. I wanted to be like you when I became a boss someday.

Many thanks to the members of my study group Goddesses of Financial Planning (GOFP), especially Joan Rossi, Kathy Longo, Dana Brewer, Kay Kramer, Janet Stanzak, Laura Kuntz, Lauri Salverda, Ellen Dubuque, and Amy Wolff. In the past eighteen years, I have always felt safe discussing challenges and have received insightful advice and feedback from you all. Without the support and wisdom of this group of women financial planners/business owners, I would not have had the confidence to start my first business in financial services in 2003 and Echo Wealth Management in 2015.

I want to thank the team at Echo Wealth Management! I am proud of what we have accomplished together, especially reaching the milestone of $100 million assets under management.

I thank my clients for trusting me and my team to be a part of their lives. I feel honored to build financial confidence for clients to pursue their passions and dreams.

I thank Michael Kitces for writing so much content over a decade to advance this profession. I have been reading your newsletter regularly and am a loyal listener of your *Financial Advisor Success* podcast.

I am grateful to know Clayton Chan, an estate attorney who has worked with me to help many clients since 2002. I always know you will give me honest and timely feedback when I come to you with questions on estate planning strategies.

I thank Cory Kiner, CPA, who is an important member of my dream team, helping me and my clients with tax planning and tax return preparation services. Tax laws are complicated, and I know I can count on you to guide me and my clients.

I want to thank the following people in my dance community: My former dance partner Jay Larson, who taught me all nineteen dances in four styles and enabled me to be a competitive ballroom dancer. My current dance partner Gene Bersten, who always dances with extreme energy that is contagious, making dancing so much fun that I will probably dance until I no longer can. My dance friends: Jacqui, Zhuojing, Adel, Shannon, Julie Ann—my life is more fun when I share this serious hobby with you all!

I bought my first piano right after September 11, 2001, and couldn't wait any longer to fulfill this childhood dream. My piano teacher and longtime friend Miroslava Kisilevitch, PhD, taught me the foundation of classical piano music. My current piano teacher, Ju-In Lin, encourages me to play for fun by choosing some popular songs after I passed the level 4 exam. You both have made me enjoy music even more.

Finally, I want to thank the dedicated team of editors, project managers, and graphic designers at Advantage Media Group|ForbesBooks, including Caren NiChartaigh, Josh Houston, Rachel Griffin, and Megan Elger, for helping me create my first book to educate and inspire more people to start financial planning now in order to own their future.

ABOUT THE AUTHOR

Echo Huang, the president and founder of Echo Wealth Management, an independent and boutique registered investment advisor (RIA) firm in Minnesota's Twin Cities, developed a passion for finance and business at a very young age. The firstborn child of two high school teachers in a small village in China, she chose to attend the Shenzhen School of Business and Economics rather than high school. By age seventeen, she had landed a sought-after job as an accountant with the Bank of China in Shenzhen. She prepared for even better opportunities by taking English classes at night, eventually quitting her job to study for the TOEFL exam and get her full-time student visa to study finance in the United States.

At age twenty, she left China, crossing the ocean with just $800 in her pocket and a yearning for adventure in her mind. Her courage and positive attitude led her to success in the business world over the next twenty years. One of her first positions was with KPMG in Minneapolis, where she worked for almost four years as a senior tax specialist. It was there that she first began to gather valuable experience in personal financial planning for corporate executives, honing a knack for incorporating stock options strategies and tax planning into individualized financial plans. Realizing that this was the professional role she was meant to play, she changed her career by becoming a financial planner in 2000, passing the Certified Financial Planner® exam in 2001.

This transition enabled Echo to provide comprehensive financial planning and investment management services in order to improve people's lives. She gained experience working in financial planning at firms both large and small in Minnesota for about fifteen years before launching Echo Wealth Management in 2015. Her passion now is helping people build the financial confidence to pursue their passions and dreams. Echo believes that holistic financial planning—synthesizing cash flow, asset allocation, investment management, retirement, insurance, and estate and tax planning together into a personalized strategic plan—forms the foundation of financial success.

Echo competes in pro-am ballroom dancing at the silver level, plays piano, practices yoga, and is a voracious reader. She also enjoys traveling around the world with her daughter, Nina. They live in Plymouth with their petite goldendoodle, Luna.

CONNECT WITH ECHO

 **www.iamechohuang.com**

echo@echowm.com

in/echohuang

@EchoHuangCFP

@EchoHuangCFP

echodancing2004